# LEARNING TO READ
# THROUGH EXPERIENCE

# LEARNING TO READ
# THROUGH EXPERIENCE

Second Edition

## Dorris M. Lee
Portland State College

## R. V. Allen
University of Arizona

APPLETON-CENTURY-CROFTS
*Educational Division*
New York MEREDITH CORPORATION

# Preface

Twenty years ago the first edition of *Learning to Read Through Experience* was published. At that time the authors stated in the preface:

Reading has always been considered the most important subject in the curriculum, particularly in the primary grades. More books have been written on the theory and practice of teaching reading than on any other subject; more research has been planned and carried through. Perhaps also more change has taken place in the methods and materials of teaching reading than in any other field.

During the past twenty years the concern for reading development has increased among parents and community as well as educators. Numerous approaches have been tried and discarded. Increasingly the emphasis of more and more people has been on the development of meaning and of reading as thinking. It is generally recognized that meaning and understanding must have their bases in the experience of the individual. Thus by providing opportunity for each child to build his own reading materials until he develops skill and confidence in handling other materials, an adequate background of experience is made implicit.

Providing for individual differences has become too often a cliché with only token implementation. Any realistic accomplishment in this direction must be based on the premise that each child should have access to materials of a wide variety

060452

in both difficulty and kind, that he should have the opportunity to deal with topics of his own concern and choose those
materials which are significant to him, and that he should have
the freedom to progress as fast and only as fast as he feels
competent to do so.

At the theoretical level the four principal aspects of the
language arts—listening, speaking, reading, and writing—
have been recognized to be different faces of the same understandings and skills. No one of these can possibly be carried
on or taught by itself; all the others are directly or implicitly
involved. The implementation of this understanding can increase the effectiveness of teaching, eliminate much confusion
of the children and result in multiple learnings. Separation of
these aspects of language arts is an adult concept which makes
school learnings seem arbitrary and incomprehensible to many
children. This of course decreases markedly the effectiveness
of such learning.

The authors have attempted to describe a plan for developing reading ability as an integral part of the development of
all the communication skills. It builds on and continues to
provide individual experiences for each child while it increases
the common group experiences. It provides for optimum development of each child through increasing his self confidence
and self direction.

D.M.L.
R.V.A.

# Contents

# LEARNING TO READ
# THROUGH EXPERIENCE

# 1

# READING AS COMMUNICATION

## COMMUNICATION SKILLS IN READING PROGRAMS

Communication skills, commonly called the language arts, occupies a larger part in the curriculum during the first twelve or thirteen years of basic education than any other curriculum element. In fact, development of communication skills begins very early in the home as the child learns to use his native language with some degree of effectiveness. Our society recognizes, however, that skillful use of the language in all its aspects requires years of instruction and practice. Ability to use language well is closely linked with success in most prestige occupations in our society. It is imperative, then, that we effectively and efficiently teach the communication skills of listening, speaking, reading and writing. This book, which focuses on learning to read through experience, implies that experiences encompassing all the language arts contribute to reading development. Some of the basic premises on which this book is developed are:

- The communication skills of listening, speaking, reading and writing are closely interrelated.

- Reading is completely interwoven with all the other language arts.

1

- Reading is concerned with words that arouse meaningful responses based on the *individual experiences* of the learner.

- Words have no inherent meaning.

- Spoken words are sound symbols which arouse meaning in the mind of the listener.

- Written words are visual symbols which, when associated with known sound symbols, arouse meaning in the mind of the reader.

- Reading is developing meaning from patterns of symbols which one recognizes and endows with meaning. *Reading arouses or calls up meanings. It does not provide them.*

*Learning to Read Through Experience* attempts to bring reading and other communication skills together in the instructional program. The point of view expressed throughout is that there is no way, nor any need, to distinguish between the reading program and other language activities. Learning to read through experience makes possible the continuing use of each child's own experience background in listening and speaking as he grows toward reading maturity.

Among those who have devoted years to study, research and development of pupil materials for use in the schools, there is widespread agreement that the communication skills are related and that the experiences of children, including their language experiences, are essential ingredients for a successful educational program. References on this topic are found in Appendix *B*.

## READING IN A FREE, DEMOCRATIC SOCIETY

It is no accident that educators are emphasizing the relatedness of communication skills and creative approaches to teaching them. The same is happening in the fields of mathematics,

science and the social sciences. Subject lines are shifting and
merging as we understand more of the process of becoming
educated in all fields. At a time when we are forced to describe
in some detail the differences in education in a free society
with an open system of education as contrasted to the authori-
tarian society with a closed system, we see creativity and diversity as distinguishing characteristics.

The closed system of education is based upon a belief that
we can *give* our children an education by passing on to them
our knowledge, scientific findings, beliefs and ideals, our systems of discovery and even our ruling passions. The rewards
of the student in a closed system are rewards for conformity.
In an open system—the one embraced by free people—we give
our children access to the colossally varied and rich learnings
of the past and present and at the same time recognize that each
child is born free to accept or reject them. Such an arrangement makes possible the unique growth of personality and
distinctive social development. It seeks to help children lift
themselves to a plane of creative expression which reaches
beyond what we have called "normal expectations." The rewards of the open system are centered in personal satisfaction.

It seems that in the past the greatest opportunity for learning in the open system has been in infancy and the preschool
years when there are few environmental demands, no curriculum and little systematic teaching. It is at this period of no
curriculum and little pressure that the greatest and most rapid
learning takes place and creativity is most universally manifest.
The open system permits originality, experimentation, inven-
tion and initiative. Its environment promotes and permits
creativity.

The purpose of studies and experimentation that have led
to a description of how children learn to read through experience is to attempt to extend an open system of education
through the primary grades in our schools. The need for creative, self-directed programs in all curriculum areas is great, but

the illustrations used here deal primarily with communication
and more specifically with reading.

The following illustration contrasts the differences in approaches to reading instruction which use the open and the
closed systems.

## CHARACTERISTIC DIFFERENCES IN TWO TYPES OF READING INSTRUCTION

| Open | Closed |
|------|--------|
| 1. Centered in the learner's recognizing that his speech can be recorded in print. | Centered in skills of reading print. |
| 2. Emphasis on developing reading skills as a part of the total language experience— the same emphasis on writing and speaking as on reading print. | Emphasis on teaching a sequence of reading skills. |
| 3. Subject matter emerges within the classroom as children record their own thinking through writing and other media. Organized skill-reading material is used to evaluate levels of achievement. | Subject matter selected and organized prior to the teaching situation. |
| 4. Reading instruction program controlled cooperatively by learners, teacher and "readers" during the learning situation. | Reading instruction program controlled by the "readers," the teacher, and other external authorities. |
| 5. Emphasis upon building habits and skills of reading as integral parts of larger experiences, especially aspects of communication. | Emphasis upon teaching specific habits and skills as separate aspects of learning. |

| Open | Closed |
|------|--------|
| 6. Emphasis on improving understandings of what reading is and how it is used in the process of learning. | Emphasis on improving methods of teaching specific habits and skills. |
| 7. Emphasis upon variability in exposures to learning situations and variability in the results expected and achieved. | Emphasis upon uniformity of learning results for minimum standards. Enrichment beyond for some. |
| 8. Judging pupil progress by observing development of self-expression, interest in reading and writing, and use of specific reading skills. | Judging pupil progress by testing ability to use specific reading skills. |

## READING CONCEPTS WHICH CHILDREN DEVELOP*

Children who learn to read through experience will not progress through a system of predetermined skills and materials. They must, however, develop certain fundamental concepts about themselves and reading so that they will have a framework on which to hang any skills they find functional and meaningful. The conceptual framework has been described as the magnet to which iron filings will fly. If the magnet is not energized, the iron filings remain motionless.

The sequence of concept development might grow something like this:

1. *What a child thinks about he can talk about.*
   Teachers begin with the thoughts of each child as the basic ingredient for developing reading skills.

* R. V. Allen, "Concept Development of Young Children in Reading Instruction," *Twenty-fourth Yearbook,* Claremont College Reading Conference (Claremont, California, 1959), pp. 12-21.

2. *What he can talk about can be expressed in painting, writing, or some other form.*

   This causes the teacher to realize that to some degree all normal children can already write and read. It cancels out any preconceived notion that a child must have a reading vocabulary of a certain size before he begins to write.

3. *Anything he writes can be read.*

   Experiences with both picture writing and with writing with the letters of our alphabet help the child to recognize that one is much more precise than the other and give the reader more specific clues about the thinking of the author.

4. *He can read what he writes and what other people write.*
The child experiences the thrill of reading what other people have written after he has experienced the thrill of seeing his own oral language take a form that can be reproduced by the process called reading.

5. *As he represents his speech sounds with symbols, he uses the same symbols (letters) over and over.*
Teaching the child to symbolize his speech sounds rather than trying to get him to assign a sound or sounds to a symbol is to take the experience approach to teaching the phonetic elements of our own language.

6. *Each letter in the alphabet stands for one or more sounds that he makes when he talks.*
At first the teacher records the oral language of the individual to develop this understanding. As the child writes on his own, this understanding matures to the point of including the many variations inherent in the English language.

7. *Every word begins with a sound that he can write down.*
Understanding how to symbolize initial sounds in words is a breakthrough to the magic realm of reading and writing.

8. *Most words have an ending sound.*
This, like the understanding above, is a normal development for children who observe speech take the form of writing.

9. *Many words have something in between.*
   This is an understanding that offers a longer-range teaching program. It continues to be a fascinating part of learning throughout the life of the individual.

10. *Some words are used over and over in our language and some words are not used very often.*
    Vocabulary control is built into the language of the individual. A few words are used hundreds of times, others only rarely.

11. *What he has to say and write is as important to him as what other people have written for him to read.*
    Many teachers have difficulty with the implementation of this understanding. However, a teacher who cannot demonstrate a real thrill over the output of ideas in his own classroom leaves out one of the principal ingredients of the formula.

12. *Most of the words he uses are the same ones which are used by other people who write for him to read.*
    Helping the child to get a built-in feeling that the main purpose of reading is to deal with the ideas of the author rather than the words he uses is a strength of the method. In effect, they read from the beginning as though they were carrying on a conversation with the author. Because they know that the story will be written in words which they use in their own speech and writing, children are released from the fear that they may not be able to read it. They are well on the way to independence in reading skills at a much earlier age that it was formerly thought possible.

As children live and learn to read in a school program which is truly an integrated, balanced program from kindergarten on, they develop more mature concepts about *what reading really is in the world about them,* such as:

- Reading is understanding and interpreting the ideas of the author.

- It is gaining new meaning by reorganization of meaning they bring to the reading.

- It is developing many types of thinking as children react in different ways: comparing, inferring, predicting, evaluating.

- It is vicarious living.

It is equally important to understand *what reading is not.*

- It is *not* saying words, but rather expressing a thought or idea, no matter how simple or how complex.

- It is *not* treating words as isolated symbols even if they follow one another in close sequence, but rather treating them as essential parts of a whole thought.

- It is *not* working one's way through a sentence by various word analysis skills, but rather relating the whole passage to express an idea after having identified any unfamiliar words through previous study.

It is hoped that children will have such a personal, satisfying experience in the early stages of reading growth that they will develop attitudes about reading, such as:

- Its values in their own lives.

- The skills they need to develop in order to achieve their reading purposes.

- The relationship of reading to thinking.

- The stimulation which reading can give to creative living.

### EVALUATING THE EXPERIENCE CURRICULUM

Teachers who propose to personalize the reading curriculum so that the thinking power of individuals is highlighted must envision and describe the bases on which such a program will be evaluated or judged. The standards for evaluation will not be as easy to describe as ones for assembly-line methods of instruction. The standards of evaluation for the experience curriculum in reading must be centered in the thinking power of individuals, their sensitivity to problems, their flexibilty in adjusting to new and different situations, their ability to make specific applications from generalizations, to make new meanings out of old ones and to take advantage of change.

The highest standards for evaluating a reading program in our society are ones which require that each child is directed toward independence in learning and confidence in his own thinking. If they do not, there is little need to try to distinguish standards for free men from those of slaves. As programs of language experience develop, the following guides should be used to judge the appropriateness of the activities and experiences:

1.  *Productive thinking is generated in the children.*
    When children learn to read through experience, the goal is not one of producing spectacular word-calling skills. The real test is that children react to reading by reconstructing the ideas of authors against a background of their own experience. They choose reading with a purpose.

2.  *Freedom of expression is allowed.*
    Activities are selected where there is no single correct response. Children develop multiple ways of saying what they have to say. In turn, they appreciate and

accept the many ways by which other people say what
they have to say.

3. *Individual talents and skills are used.*
Children develop confidence as independent workers.
The reading curriculum is personalized as well as individualized. There is an expectancy that each child can
search in his own storehouse of experiences to solve
reading problems which are meaningful to him. The
slow-learning child, the emotionally disturbed, and the
"immature" make significant progress in a program
where their own ideas are *valued* and *used*. The gifted
child may have the opportunity to come closer to developing his potential, especially in the expression of his
own ideas.

4. *Thinking is modified as children add new learnings.*
This is in contrast to fixed-answer problem solving
which is promoted in many worksheets and workbooks
children are required to complete. In the experience
curriculum, the emphasis is on the child's developing
new material which reflects his use of new learnings.

5. *Curiosity is satisfied through exploration.*
Children are not always expected to accept other people's answers and solutions. There must be as high value
set on *not* accepting answers as on the ability to repeat
and record the answers of others.

6. *Personal discipline is practiced as children are freed to
work productively.*
When children have a responsibility for selecting their
reading material and pacing their skill development, a
type of discipline is required which has always been
associated with creative workers. Their ability to discipline themselves in any learning experience is a mark
of growth toward self-direction.

7. *Personal satisfaction is achieved by the learner.*
This personal satisfaction is above and beyond that which comes from success on standardized tests where ideal performance is conformity to the examiner's norms, to his standards of excellence, his criteria of desirable

or even usual behavior. Personal satisfaction in the experience curriculum is the result of pursuing self-accepted goals with best efforts. Such efforts result in enthusiasm and make a contribution to independent learning.

The reading program which is based on the learner's experience should reflect the goals of a society which values creativity and divergent thinking. Learning experiences are selected which generate productive thinking, allow freedom of expression, stimulate individuality, value ingenuity, satisfy curiosity and promote personal satisfaction to the extent that learning to read is a lifelong experience which requires ever maturing and more complex skills and knowledge.

# 2

# GAUGING A CHILD'S DEVELOPMENT

How can we tell when a child has developed to the point where he is ready to read language symbols? Just because a child is not yet in school, or because he is in the first grade, or because he is six, or he is seven does not provide us with the answer. It is trite to say that children are different, yet we have only begun to make constructive use of this fact in our schools.

Groups of 25 to 30 children arrive in our kindergarten or first grade classrooms in the fall for the first time. We know very little if anything about them.

About all we know when a child enters school is that:

1. He has had about five or six years of experience in living.

2. His experiences have been different from those of any other child—but similar in many ways.

3. The better we understand the learning development these experiences have produced, the better we can guide his next steps in learning development.

4. His differences from other children can be strengths and we need to see how to take advantage of them.

5. His differences may also reveal needed areas of learning development.

6. As with anyone at any stage, learning development can only occur through that individual's own experience, real or vicarious, as he perceives (sees) it and reacts to it.

7. We must plan experiences for children which will move them from where they are in the direction of greater understanding and control of themselves and the world in which they live.

Even when we believe firmly in the importance of planning to take utmost advantage of differences in children we feel uncertain as to how this is best accomplished. The first and obvious step is to discover what these differences are, and the means of doing this is also quite unclear. First, we must feel thoroughly justified in spending considerable time and energy discovering where each child is in various phases of his development and in persisting in this analysis as a continuous program. The experiences we will be using are good experiences for children, a part of a continuous process of learning development, and the kinds of activities which are desirable for the child under any circumstances. It is not a period of waiting, of only collecting data to find out what to do. Rather it is one of providing increasingly good learning experiences based on increasing understanding of individual children and their needs. Let us explore some of the more useful ways in which we can find out about children. No teacher will use all of these with all children but general evaluations of each child will point up kinds of exploration which are particularly important.

## OBSERVATION

Observation is always available to teachers. The problem lies in being aware of what is significant to observe and how to record what we see. In general there are two kinds of observations, those in a free and unstructured situation and those in a situation planned, partly at least, for the purpose of finding out how certain children react under specific circumstances. The first might be in free activity either in the classroom or on the school grounds, or it might be out of school. The second can be any one of an almost unlimited number of situations depending on what the teacher wishes to find out. For instance, she may set up a group for painting with brushes and tempera but where there is one less brush than there are children in the group. She then settles down nearby with another group with the understanding that those in this first group are not to contact her till she is free. Here she may observe the way children react to a problem. Who gives up? Who takes the initiative to find a solution? Who blows up? Who demands his rights regardless of others? Who finds a satisfying alternative while waiting his turn? Who needs adult assistance or decision so much that he contacts the teacher in spite of instructions to the contrary? Many other observations may be made depending on what occurs.

These observations may show much about each child's self-concept and his emotional maturity, two very important factors which need to be taken into account in planning his learning. General areas for observation may be listed:*

1. Is the child's life comfortable enough so that he can give attention to school learnings?

    a. Does he show any evidence of physical ill health?

        (1) Excessive thinness; excessive overweight; very small or very large in body build for age; pallor; weary expression; poor posture; dark circles or puffiness under eyes.

        (2) Acts tired or apathetic; is easily irritated; makes frequent trips to toilet; has persistent nervous habits.

---

* See Appendix *C* for a condensed version of the Observation Chart which may be duplicated for teachers' use.

such as muscular twitching or biting of nails or lips; is subject to spasms, fainting spells, or frequent nosebleeds; gets short of breath after mild exertion and climbing stairs; lacks appetite; vomits frequently; has frequent accidents.

(3) Doesn't want to play; has aches or pains; feels dizzy.

(4) Frequent or long-continued colds; persistent nasal discharge; breathes persistently through mouth.

(5) Rashes or inflamed skin areas; boils; hives; many accidental injuries, such as cuts, scratches, bruises, burns.

(6) Limping gait, dragging of foot, spastic gait, waddling gait, walking on the toes or heels, walking on the inner or outer borders of feet.

(7) Habitually standing with toes pointed in (pigeon toes) or out; standing with ankles rolled inward; heels of shoes worn down on the inside or outside in a short time; complaints of pains in the feet or legs; reporting of corns, bunions, blisters, or calluses on balls of feet; bow legs; knock knees.

(8) Upper back humped (kyphosis); lower back hollow (lordosis); round shoulders; one shoulder considerably higher than the other; complaints of backache; chest abnormally high; hollow-chested; narrow-chested; arms and hands limp or flaccid; deformities of fingers; head abnormally large; wryneck (head tilted to side).

*b.* Does he show evidence of mental ill health?

(1) Is his attention frequently not on the immediate happenings?

(2) Does he daydream frequently?

(3) Does he lack normal response to teacher or children?

(4) Does he usually stay apart from others in the room? on the playground?

(5) Is he frequently involved in his own activities or activities with others which are unrelated to the ongoing situation?

(6) Is he continuously jumping from one thing to another?

c. Does he show high anxiety, tension, unhappiness?

(1) Is he easily irritated or upset?

(2) Is he often afraid?

(3) Does he often become overexcited?

(4) Is it difficult for him to withhold or modify judgment?

(5) Is his world largely blacks and whites with few grays?

(6) Does he become jealous easily?

2. Are his "intake" senses functioning adequately?

a. Are there evidences of inadequate vision?

(1) Does he react inadequately to or avoid activities which require distant vision? which require close vision?

(2) Does he frequently frown, rub his eyes, close one eye or tilt his head when trying to see?

(3) Do his eyes or lids show abnormal conditions?

b. Are there evidences of inadequate hearing?

(1) Does he frequently fail to respond?

(2) Does he often ask, "What?" or "What did you say"?

(3) Does he frequently watch and imitate others whether appropriate or not?

(4) Does he hear variations in sounds?

    *c.* Are there evidences of inadequate physical participation?

        (1) Does he fail to show normal curiosity?

        (2) Does he fail to explore new situations or new materials by touching, feeling, smelling, tasting?

    *d.* To what kinds of things does he fail to give attention?

        (1) Do certain kinds of things tend to be ignored more than others?

        (2) Are there some which he always sees, hears, and pays attention to?

3. Are his "expressive" abilities functioning adequately?

    *a.* Does he express himself in complete thought units?

    *b.* Is his expression relevant to the topic?

    *c.* Does he contribute to group discussion and chart stories?

    *d.* Does he converse freely?

    *e.* Does he enunciate clearly and correctly?

    *f.* Does he use good English?

4. Are school learnings important to him?

    *a.* What is known of parent's goals, values?

        (1) What is their educational level?

        (2) What is their occupational level?

        (3) What are their aspirations and anticipations for the child?

            (*a*) Evidence, direct and indirect.

    *b.* Does he choose to look at books?

        (1) Does he find satisfaction in them?

        (2) Does he refer to content of books as a resource?

    *c.* Does he show normal curiosity about the world around him?

        (1) Does he explore the rich environment of the classroom?

        (2) Does he bring in materials, objects and ideas which are related to some aspect of the classroom environment?

        (3) Does he ask questions or make statements which indicate normal curiosity and concern with understanding more about objects and materials in the classroom?

    *d.* What kinds of activities hold his attention?

        (1) What kinds elicit short attention span?

        (2) Do his free comments concern mostly in-school topics and materials? or out-of-school topics and materials?

        (3) Are his wishes and wants school-related or not?

5. Does he see himself as able to successfully accomplish school learnings?

    *a.* What does evidence of self-concept show?

        (1) Does he volunteer for anything? for new things?

        (2) Does he balk at trying new things?

        (3) Does he tackle each task with confidence? or does he attempt to delay beginning it by stalling or by finding other things to do?

        (4) Do his statements about his accomplishments give clues to his concept of his abilities?

        (5) Does he quickly lose interest in activities particularly when he meets some failure?

    *b.* Does his self-confidence vary in different areas?

        (1) Does he show more confidence and self-direction out of the classroom than in? more in certain types of classroom activities than in others?

## OBJECTIVE MEASUREMENT

Objective measurement tends to be more difficult and less reliable the younger and the less school-oriented the child. Certain objective measurements, however, are adequate and helpful both to check the validity of observations and to extend beyond where observation is useful.

    1. Measurement of physical development is particularly advantageous.

        *a. Vision.* The *Snellen Chart* must be recognized as only the crudest and most preliminary of measuring instruments. It gives indication of vision only of objects of a certain size at a certain distance, 20 feet, which is not the distance at which most school learnings are seen. Those who fail the test certainly need the attention of specialists but perhaps not as much as many who pass the tests. It eliminates no one from the need for further checks.

        Among the factors which need to be tested are muscle imbalance, fusion.

        *b. Hearing.* Measurement of hearing includes the whisper test and the watch test. Of the two the latter is much to be preferred since the level and pitch of the sound is always the same. It is essential to control conflicting sounds during such a test. The watch test is, however, quite inadequate for testing hearing and locates only a portion of those needing attention.

        Volume and distance of sound are not as important in many cases as pitch since ability to hear sounds of dif-

ferent pitch varies considerably across the hearing range.
Audiometers are a far superior measuring device and can
be used with a group as soon as they can write numbers
which they hear.

c. *General physical maturity* can be measured but it is not yet
feasible to do it for all children. The most usual method
is by X-ray of the wrist bones and interpretation must be
made by a specialist.

2. Measurements of mental development need to be used with
caution.

a. *Reliability of paper and pencil tests.* Individual tests are
not financially feasible except for special cases. Group
tests with five and six-year-olds need to be evaluated with
various factors in mind: the goodness of the communication in a situation unfamiliar to children, the adequacy of
school skills such as handling booklets, using pencils for
specific purposes, concentration on his own test blank
only, and the ability to follow precise directions. The
timed test possesses an additional problem of keeping
young children working effectively within the time limits.
Observation of the testing situation can give some basis
for judging the reliability of the test scores for the group.
Also individuals can be identified whose scores probably
do not represent a true measure.

b. *Validity of mental tests.* If we are looking for a figure which
will tell us the child's general mental ability we will not
be able to find it. The so-called intelligence test measures
a certain few of the child's intellectual abilities. These
abilities are ones which seemed to have the greatest relationship with success in school work where in general
such success depends on doing well on teacher-assigned
tasks. The usual tests do not measure self-directive abilities, motivation or the creative abilities which are beginning to be recognized as highly valuable.

c. *Kinds of tests available.* *

 (1) Group tests of general intelligence:

  (a) *California Test of Mental Maturity,* Kgn-1, gives separate language and nonlanguage scores.

  (b) *Cattell Intelligence Test Scale 1,* nonverbal.

  (c) *Davis-Eells Test of General Intelligence and Problem Solving Ability,* no reading required, grades 1-2.

  (d) *Goodenough Draw-a-Man Test,* Kgn-3.

  (e) *Group Test of Learning Capacity: Dominion Tests,* Kgn-1.

  (f) *IPAT Culture Free Intelligence Test,* ages 4-8.

  (g) *Kuhlmann-Anderson Intelligence Tests,* Sixth Edition, Kgn-1.

  (h) *Lorge-Thorndike Intelligence Tests,* Kgn-1, non-verbal.

  (i) *SRA Primary Mental Abilities Test,* Kgn-2.

 (2) Tests of "reading readiness" which measure those specific factors having greatest relationship to learning to read, especially by the basal reader approach:

  (a) *American School Reading Readiness Test.*

  (b) *Group Test of Reading Readiness: The Dominion Tests.*

  (c) *Lee-Clark Reading Readiness Test,* 1951 Revision.

  (d) *Metropolitan Readiness Tests.*

---

* See Appendix *D* for data needed in obtaining any of the following tests.

(3) Tests which measure kinds of abilities which are thought of as creative are not readily available but have now been described in several sources.* Their value and significance is still uncertain. Teachers who would like to use these measures as a part of a program in developing divergent and productive thinking could have a very rewarding experience.

## INFORMAL MEASUREMENT

There are numerous means of informal measurement of factors important for success in a school program. Many are extensions of observation.

1. The extent of perception and differentiation in the way children see their environment is evident in their pictures. The amount of detail and indications of understanding of relationship and function can often be seen. For example, a drawing of a figure with only lines for head, body, arms and legs shows less maturity than one which includes neck, shoulders, hands, knees, feet and features of the face. Also differentiation of doors from windows and paths leading from doorways show more understanding than indiscriminate rectangles placed on or partly on a house.

2. A measure of a child's verbal development is a record of his language recorded as he dictates. As each child dictates his story and the teacher records it without question or correction, an objective evidence of language ability is available. Successive recording over a period of time can indicate the extent of progress as well as areas of little progress, pinpointing need.

* E. Paul Torrance, *Guiding Creative Talent* (Englewood Cliffs, New Jersey, Prentice-Hall, 1962), 278 p. Jacob W. Getzels and Philip W. Jackson, *Creativity and Intelligence* (New York, Wiley, 1962), 293 p.

3. Characteristics of creativity have been listed by various research workers and these give leads for both observation and informal measurement. Lowenfeld* has listed the following:

- *Sensitivity to problems.* Awareness of defects, needs or deficiencies; perceiving the odd or unusual in situations; refinement of the senses, including heightened awareness of social responsibility, and the ability to identify with the problem or experience.

- *Fluency of ideas.* Ideational and associational volubleness in sensory and verbal performances.

- *Flexibility.* Freedom from inertia of thought; spontaneous shift of set; adapting and utilizing the new process or product of the ever shifting experience or thought to more satisfying ends.

- *Originality.* Production of uncommon responses; production of remote, unusual, unconventional associations; cleverness.

- *Analysis and the ability to abstract.* Abstracting the details from the whole.

- *Synthesis and closure.* The process of combining several elements to form a new whole; closure of several objects or parts.

- *Redefinition and the ability to rearrange.* Shifting the function of objects and using them in a new way so as to give new meaning.

- *Coherence of organization.* More complete integration of thinking, feeling, and perceiving through economy of effort; aesthetically organized or harmonized relationships.

* Adapted from Victor Lowenfeld, "Current Research on Creativity," *NEA Journal,* Vol. 47 (November, 1958), pp. 538-540.

## COMPARISON OF EVIDENCE FROM OBSERVATION AND MEASUREMENT

When conclusions reached by observation confirm testing results we can be more sure of our judgments concerning the child's present stage of development. This does not necessarily indicate the child's rate of future growth, particularly if his situation is changed. One reason for the often observed steady growth rate is that the situation for most children does not change markedly from year to year. For any specific individual the developmental pattern can not be assured and this fact must be recognized. Beginning school, where the program is one which provides successful learning and challenging experiences for each child, may well step up the rate of development. Unhappily, an impoverished and rigid program which takes minimal account of individual needs can as readily depress the rate of development.

When testing results and evidence from observation are inconsistent, one or the other or both must be questioned. There are a number of steps that can be taken:

1. Continue observations, but *not* to find evidence to prove or disprove either previous observations or test results. We should never observe to prove a point but merely observe to find out. The tests used and/or the child's response to the tests may have been inadequate. The observations may have been inadequate in range or choice of situations or may have been made with preconceived expectations of results. Or it may simply be that the behavior observed was misinterpreted.

It may be that further information is needed from other sources such as conference with parents and others who have had significant contact with the child.

Another possibility which is a frequent cause of inconsistent information is the emotional-social problems of children which affect their perceptions of situations. We see a situation in a certain way but the child may see it quite differently and reacts to it, of course, as *he* sees it not as *we* do. But we interpret according to our perceptions. For instance, we may feel we are providing a child with an opportunity for learning and giving him help with it. He may see it as a threatening situation, since he has tried before and failed and so sees our "help" as pressure to do what he doesn't dare try. Some of the classroom procedures which children may well see as threatening are:

- Two reading groups each day for those who can't read.

- Developing of word-recognition skills prior to listening-speaking skills.

- Sending children out of room for "special help" from speech therapist, remedial reading teacher, or others.

Since he accomplishes little or nothing our interpretation is that he cannot learn, whereas the test results indicate he can. Better-conceived learning experiences well might enable him to increase his learning development greatly.

2. Retest. This may be done with a second form of the same test, or with a different test. Where possible, individual tests may be given, especially if preliminary attempts to come to a consistent decision have not been successful. The most commonly used individual tests are the *Revised Stanford Binet Scale* and the *Wechsler Intelligence Scale for Children*. Both of these require highly and specifically trained personnel to administer and interpret them. Since the testor achieves rapport and communication with the child before testing can begin, one major problem of group testing is overcome.

### WHAT DO WE DO ABOUT IT?

Now that we have a great deal of knowledge about children which we have been putting to use as it was discovered, what does it mean for our program? Much learning has been going on along with the exploration and information gathering. Backgrounds have been enriched through the planned experiences. Relationships have been developing as children worked and played together. The classroom has been established as a friendly and comfortable though exciting and challenging place to live and work.

By this time we have carefully kept records on each child. We undoubtedly will not have all the information suggested for each child, but we will have considered thoughtfully each general area. The records may be set up on cards or in loose leaf notebooks or in any other way which provides flexibility in adding information, plans and questions throughout the year. We have an estimate of each child's development which includes (1) his strengths and abilities and (2) his areas of needs. This must be kept up to date continually as the child develops.

The first step at this point is to look at each child as a total person, trying to understand him better as an individual, why he reacts the way he does and how he might be expected to react under various situations.

The next step is to plan experiences which will use strengths and develop abilities in the areas of need. This must be done for each child but it does not mean that each child will be working alone on his own program. Such a procedure would lose many important values. Rather, children will be working together according to specific needs for the purpose of meeting these needs. As an individual child accomplishes steps in development he moves to other groups which are working on the tasks he needs to tackle next. So groups ebb and flow. Children are always working at each one's growing edge and always on something each specifically needs.

There are no slow groups or fast groups. Rather there are friendship groups which are flexibly arranged so that children may learn from each other as well as from the teacher. There is never consistently a range wide enough that either discouragement or false confidence results. Instead each is developing needed learnings in all appropriate areas. The following chapters give much more specific help in planning such a program.

# 3

## LANGUAGE EXPERIENCES IN READING DEVELOPMENT

All children who enter our schools have had experiences which form a basis for extending their reading experiences. Many of them are unaware of the fact that they have already been reading many things in their environment and that they can read some things in print, especially those things that they have seen so often on television and in advertising.

*They can read the:*

| | |
|---|---|
| weather | is it hot or cold?<br>is it wet or dry?<br>is it windy or calm? |
| plants | are they green or brown?<br>are they dead or alive?<br>are they large or small? |
| time of day | is it early or late?<br>is it morning or afternoon?<br>is it dark or light? |
| faces of people | are they happy or sad?<br>are they smiling or frowning?<br>are they serious or joking? |
| texture | is it smooth or rough?<br>is it fuzzy or prickly? |

*They can read:*

colors, size, shape, feeling, action.

*Most of them can read:*

signs on the way to school, popular brands as advertised on television programs, names of stores in shopping centers.

*A few can read:*

their names, labels in the classroom, and simple picture captions that are obvious.

*Occasionally one can read:*

simple stories and anything which he has dictated as a story.

Most children have been made to feel that it is important for them to learn to read printed material and they are willing to do the necessary study to achieve this goal as long as they understand what they are doing. For this reason it is essential that teachers place major emphasis on activities which help each child to learn to read through his experience. Although most experiences in life have a relationship to the process of reading, especially from the aspect of giving meanings to reading, the material in this chapter emphasizes the language experiences which make significant contributions to the reading process.

## A SEQUENCE OF LANGUAGE EXPERIENCES IN READING DEVELOPMENT

Throughout the child's school experience there is opportunity and need to help him improve his language power through listening, speaking, reading, and writing. To do this, the child goes through a sequence of experiences which are designed to enrich his background and improve his skills. *The goals of increased learnings and better skills* cannot be separated in an effective, efficient instructional program. To attempt to do so is to ask the child to do at an early age one of the most difficult tasks of the scholar—to integrate learnings into meaningful behavior. To take reading out of its rightful place in the total language experience program is to ask children to do what is impossible for many of them. Or it requires the teacher to use valuable time to put back together what did not need to be separated out in the first place.

Teachers can achieve their goals of reading instruction in many ways. Some of them require that reading be brought out for special attention—to the neglect of other facets of language development. Other teachers are able to leave reading in its natural place and work to develop skills in all facets of language experience at the same time and with equal emphasis.

The following description suggests the basic language experiences and some illustrative activities which will maintain the "togetherness" of language in communication and at the same time help children to achieve reading skills commensurate with their needs and abilities. The steps in the sequence are not discrete ones which must follow one after the other, but they do give the teacher some direction in growing from the least mature to the more mature skills. The teacher is helped in using this guide to experiences and activities if he remembers that one *never finishes with any of the basic experiences.* Each one has been selected after careful study to insure that every basic experience is one that must be studied over a period of years and that it is useful throughout life. Since all the steps cannot be introduced at one time or during one school year, they are described below in a sequence that can be followed with give and take in both directions.

The instructional level of an individual can be determined by informal observations which will locate the step or group of steps in the sequence given in the overview that follows.

If a teacher observes that a child has too much difficulty in trying to dictate something, she would judge that the child needs guidance and added skill in sharing experiences, discussion experiences and listening to and telling stories before any emphasis is made on skills in dictating. A child who is reluctant to try reading from the easiest kind of books would be judged to need more experience in writing down his own speech, in developing a sight vocabulary of common words and of adding to his sight vocabulary words which are of special interest to him.

As the teacher works with individuals and groups in the extension of skills, he must remember that steps where a measure of independence has been achieved need continuing exercise. *None is ever finished!* The more difficult and complex skills cannot be dealt with effectively unless the child has considerable skill and independence with the language experiences requiring less maturity.

An overview of the major language experiences which are required for effective communication in a democratic society follows. These major language experiences in reading development were identified and described during a five-year reading study project in San Diego County, California.* Following the overview is a more detailed description of the language experiences for beginning reading stages (pp. 36-69).

## AN OVERVIEW OF LANGUAGE EXPERIENCES IN READING

1. *Sharing Experiences.* The ability to tell or illustrate something on a purely personal basis.

2. *Discussion Experiences.* The ability to interact with what other people say and write.

* Department of Education, San Diego County, California, Reading Study Project, *Improving Reading Instruction* (1961), Monographs 1-4.

3. *Listening to Stories.* The ability to hear what others have to say and relate it to one's own experiences.

4. *Telling Stories.* The ability to organize one's thinking so that it can be shared orally or through dictation in a clear and interesting manner.

5. *Dictating.* The ability to choose, from all that might be said, the most important part for someone else to write and read.

6. *Developing Speaking, Writing, Reading Relationships.* The ability to conceptualize reading as speech that has been written.

7. *Making and Reading Books.* The ability to organize one's ideas into a form that others can use. Also, the ability to use the ideas which others have shared through books.

8. *Developing Awareness of Common Vocabulary.* The ability to recognize that our language contains many common words and patterns of expression.

9. *Expanding Vocabulary.* The ability to expand one's vocabulary through listening and speaking, followed by writing and reading.

10. *Writing Independently.* The ability to write one's own ideas and present them in a form for others to read.

11. *Reading Whole Books.* The ability to read books for information, recreation, and improvement of reading skills on an individualized basis.

12. *Improving Style and Form.* The ability to profit from listening to and reading well written materials.

13. *Using a Variety of Resources.* The ability to recognize and use many resources in expanding vocabulary, improving oral and written expression, and sharing.

14. *Reading a Variety of Symbols.* The ability to read symbols in their total environment—clock, calendar, radio dial, thermometer.

15. *Studying Words.* The ability to find the correct pronunciation and meaning of words and to spell the words in writing activities.

16. *Improving Comprehension.* The ability, through oral and written activities, to gain skill in following directions, understanding words in the context of sentences and paragraphs, reproducing the thought in a passage, reading for general significance.

17. *Outlining.* The ability to use various methods of briefly restating ideas in the order in which they were written or spoken.

18. *Summarizing.* The ability to get the main impression, outstanding idea, or the details of what has been read or spoken.

19. *Integrating and Assimilating Ideas.* The ability to use reading and listening for specific purposes of a personal nature.

20. *Reading Critically.* The ability to determine the validity and reliability of statements.

These language experiences become the major framework within which children learn to read through experience. When conceptualized as a program much bigger than "the reading period," the development of these language experiences gives depth of meaning to art and construction activities; it is the vehicle for conveying meanings of social studies emphases, of science experiences, of describing quantitative aspects of the environment; it builds spirit and understanding into singing of songs and playing of games; it places the "creative thinking process" at the heart of the instructional program.

### Sharing Experiences

The teacher helps each child to gain confidence in oral and written expression (painting and drawing) which represents his own thinking. Sharing experiences may or may not be related to ongoing themes and units in the classroom. The important concept for the teacher to hold is that every time a student takes the responsibility for sharing his ideas, orally, through painting or through writing, he is developing his own concept of self, classifying his thoughts and increasing his ability to communicate them, and extending his feelings of responsibility as a group member.

Young children enjoy bringing things from home—treasures and tales of out-of-school experiences. Just the showing of what he has brought may be all that the timid child can do at first. Later he will respond to the teacher's questions with a word or short phrase. Still later he will face the group and make his contribution by himself.

Many children are able and anxious to do oral sharing from the beginning of school. These children should be helped to improve their oral sharing and encouraged to find many ways to share their ideas, their experiences, and their feelings. They should also assume some responsibility for sharing news items and ideas of other people which they have found helpful or interesting to them. Improvement can be effectively stimulated by group evaluation of the sharing period where the main emphasis is appreciation and approval for progress toward group-established goals. Teacher's comments which recognize growth and development too subtle for children to see are also very effective.

Some children enjoy publishing their own newspapers and magazines as a means of sharing the news, their stories, poetry, puzzles, comics, games, and information. If the teacher provides a few samples of children's magazines, plans for time for writing and publishing, and provides space for an office, the children will do publications such as described in Chapter 5.

Many children can share their ideas and experiences by painting and then telling or writing about the painting. A news bulletin board can be provided so children can share by putting items on the board for all to read.

The important thing to remember is that there should be opportunity daily in every classroom for some sharing experience. This provides the openness, the motivation, the main ideas upon which other language experiences are developed. These experiences characterize the difference in education in a free society and in a closed society. They emphasize the value of individual contributions.

**Developing Discussion Skills**

As children develop skill in sharing ideas and experiences of a random nature, the teacher should begin to develop within the classroom an environment which expands the interest of many children. This planned environment should result in the development of a talking-listening situation with interaction between pupils and between the teacher and children. These situations require that a child who has made one contribution must alter any subsequent contribution by what has transpired in between. This requires that each participant listen carefully to what others are saying as the discussion centers around a *theme*.

Discussion skills are more mature ones than those required when a person shares an idea without any relation to what others have said. They are more mature in their requirements on the individual than skills developed in answering questions. They give opportunity for the use of wide-range vocabulary. There is created a learning situation in which there is a great deal of repetition of key words to express the ideas of the *theme*. At the same time there is abundant opportunity for listening to and saying words which are of highest frequency in our language.

Planning for a developmental program of discussion experiences might be done as follows: The teacher brings into the classroom pictures, objects, books, and other material that suggest the interests of many children. As she talks about these things, she asks questions which engage children in talking with her and with each other about the topic.

At least once each week there should be time scheduled for a discussion around a *topic* or *theme*. These discussions should be for the purpose of improving discussion techniques. As the children engage in discussing the topics, they can gradually evolve their own standards for participation. Most groups will decide that a person should:

- Talk only when he has something to say or a question to ask which will clarify the discussion or carry it forward.

- Speak so he can be easily understood.

- Use increasingly effective language.

- Back points of discussion with evidence when necessary.

- Listen with an open mind to what others have to say.

- Weigh opinions of others.

- Be willing to change his mind when he thinks another idea is better.

- Be courteous, even when he disagrees.

- Be thoughtful of the need for many people to participate in the discussion.

As the standards for discussion evolve, the teacher has an opportunity to lead the children to another great discovery— that when a person reads, he is having a silent discussion with another person, the author. He must be willing and able to treat authorship with the same skills he uses in a discussion. Children who are able to write with ease might work to improve their skills in discussion between two or more persons by (1) selecting any common word such as "ocean," "airplane," "war," "glass"; (2) naming two or more characters and (3) beginning with the characters talking on the topic selected.

## Listening to Stories

The teacher who is helping children learn to read through experience provides time for them to hear stories each day. The reading may be done by the teacher or by a child who has been invited in from another classroom. The principal might be invited to read to the children something he likes.

As stories are read aloud, children are able to call to memory their own everyday experiences, their imaginations are heightened, their hopes and desires are stimulated, they project themselves into fuller ranges of thought and their interests are broadened.

The quality of original paintings of children is greatly influenced by the quality and variety of material selected for oral reading in the classroom. By hearing the teacher or some other person read aloud lovely poems and stories, there is developed in the heart and mind of children a sympathy for ideas expressed and a desire for self-expression. Within such an environment, every child is sure to bring out his own thoughts through speech or painting. This attitude and desire is a major goal of the experience approach to reading. Without it the approach is as dull and meaningless as any other approach which fails to involve the learner as a thinking individual with opportunities for individual self-expression.

When listening to stories being read is a part of the planned language-experience sequence, it is more than entertainment and recreation. It is a means of broadening interests and extending concepts. It is a period of vocabulary enrichment and the maturing of sentence sense. It is an essential language experience in the improvement of story telling.

To vary the story reading experiences for young children, the teacher might invite older children, librarians, and parents to read from time to time. If there are older children in the school who write well, they might be invited to read their original compositions.

Books should be selected which assure a balance between the

- real and imaginary
- biography and autobiography
- prose and poetry
- sense and nonsense
- conversation and description
- animals and people.

Children should be guided in their listening to hear things other than the story itself. Listening can be varied by such activities as listening for the

- beginning of sentences
- words that tell "how big" and "how little"
- words that tell the color of things, sounds, shapes, and speed
- passages that have good description
- questions and exclamations.

## Telling Stories

The telling of stories is as important as listening to them. It is a more creative experience and develops contact with an audience which few language experiences can do. This contact encourages a greater output of language embellishments, sound effects, physical movements, and voice inflections.

Story telling offers real experience in expressing ideas in thought units, in using colorful and descriptive language, in developing ideas in sequence and in choosing good action words. All of these are essential experiences for children to take to "print reading" if they are going to be able to read with meaning and interpret what they have read.

Story telling in its simplest form is an essential step in moving into the dictating of stories and then to independent writing. It should be a daily experience in classrooms. Following are some suggested procedures:

- The teacher can tell stories, real or imaginary.

- A child can tell a story, usually after he has had time to prepare.

- The story may be like one he has heard or read or it may be purely imaginary.

- The teacher can start a story and let it grow as different children add to it.

- When a group of children makes a story which they like very much, the teacher can help them develop it into a picture story. Responsibility for illustrating different scenes and events can be divided among the children.

- Children should learn how to tell stories clearly enough so that others can dramatize the story as it goes along. This can be done through a pantomime technique in which (1) a child knows well in advance that he can select a story to tell, (2) on the day the story is to be told, the story teller selects children to represent the various characters, (3) the classroom is arranged so there is plenty of stage room for the characters, who are hearing the story for the first time, to act out their parts.

- Children who paint pictures might have an opportunity to tell stories which relate to their pictures. Such an oral experience tends to stimulate better expression when the child is at the easel.

### Dictating

A child cannot be expected to make progress in the more technical aspects of communication until such time as he can give *clear oral expression to his own ideas.* The recording of ideas can take numerous forms. Some which are especially good for class groups are painting and dictating. In using painting to record ideas, the child continues to employ skills learned early at school. To make the ideas portrayed in the painting meaningful to others, oral or written language must be added. In the kindergarten and first grade the child dictates the stories and the teacher records the story to accompany the painting. Some dictation is taken individually, some within a small group with children arranged so they can observe the writing and occasionally the teacher takes dictation from a child while the total class observes the writing.

As children dictate their own ideas to an "adult reader," they are developing a fundamental concept about "what reading is." They can see for themselves that it is speech written down. As the child sees his own speech taking the form of writing, he is beginning to develop lifelong skills in both reading and writing. He is beginning to understand the real basis of all reading material. At the same time, most children begin to recognize printed symbols for words which they have produced through speech.

The teacher, recognizing that each child brings to school a language personality which is different from every other one in the classroom, determines to preserve that individual personality at the same time that certain understandings and skills are being habituated. To do this, the procedure from the first requires the individual to express his own thoughts, ideas, aspirations and ideals. This the child does through speaking, painting, writing and other means. The teacher works with individual contributions to help the child move from oral and pictorial expression of his ideas to expression through writing.

As the child dictates, or writes, he reads—not only what *he* writes but what *other* children write. There is no control on the vocabulary except the control which is inherent in the children themselves. The following procedure has been used success-fully:

1. The teacher asks children to express their ideas—something they are thinking about, have observed, heard about, wished for, etc.—with simple crayon drawings.

2. Eight to ten children are asked to work with the teacher at one time. The teacher sits at a table where she can write and has the children stand around her in such a way that they can observe her write.

3. One by one the children tell something about their pictures. From the "talk" the teacher helps the child extract one or two important things which she writes down while all the children observe.

4. While writing the teacher talks informally with the children about:

- words

- names of letters

- beginning sounds

- ending sounds

- sounds in between.

She proves to the children that anything they say can be written down with letters in our alphabet and that a person who knows how to read can tell exactly what they said without hearing them.

5. The stories of each group are bound into books with construction paper covers. The children are treated as authors of books that other people can read and enjoy. The books may be named by children in each group.

6. The day following the making of a book, the same group that made it can be invited to look at the book. Depending on the maturity and past experiences of the children involved, they can be helped to recall what was recorded and

*Department of Education, San Diego County, California*

to find words that are alike, words that begin alike, words that begin like their names, etc.

7. On another day the teacher may invite a group to read with her a book they did not write. This is especially valuable if some children are able to recognize a few words. They begin to see that they can read what other people have written for them to read.

8. Place the books in a reading center for the children to enjoy and for them to use as reference for spelling after they begin their own writing.

9. After one experience of taking dictation in small groups, begin taking dictation with easel paintings as described in "Writing Independently" (see pages 66-67).

10. As soon as most of the children have had an opportunity to contribute to some books and have dictated at least one story with an easel painting, begin using incomplete sentences (see pages 61-63).

### Developing Speaking, Writing, Reading Relationships

The natural way for a child to understand "what reading really is" is to observe the recording of his own speech and the speech of others with the letters of the alphabet. The sounds that are produced through speech are reproduced by symbols which are selected by the writer to represent the sounds. In the kindergarten and early first grade the teacher engages in "chit-chat" which relates to the problem of helping children understand that what they say can make reading material. The purpose is not to develop specific word recognition skills. Actually, all that is being done is to help each child conceptualize reading in a simple framework such as:

- What he thinks about he can talk about.

- What he can talk about can be expressed in painting, story telling, writing or some other form.

- What is written can be read.

- The books we read are merely what the author would say to us.

The procedure of representing speech sounds with symbols places phonics in its true and natural role as an aid to language development. It is opposite from the widely used procedure of taking a sequence of predetermined symbols and matching sound symbols to them.

If any specific word recognition skills are developed in the early stages of instruction, *they must emerge as a natural lan-*

*guage experience.* The technical aspects must be subjugated to a role of helping to support the major purposes. They must be taught when the individual is having personal language experiences which require their application. Some word recognition skills which might emerge from some children, but not all, during kindergarten and first grades are:

- Ability to recognize words that are alike, words that begin alike, words that end alike.

- Ability to use names of the letters of the alphabet in talking about words.

- Ability to recognize one's name in print.

- Ability to write one's name on paintings and other personal productions.

- Ability to write and read with independence many of the words of highest frequency in our language.

- Skill in selecting the alphabet symbols for initial sounds and endings of words not in the sight vocabulary but in the speaking vocabulary.

- Ability to recognize some high frequency words in any reading material in his environment.

- Ability to pronounce and read meaningfully words that are familiar in speech but unfamiliar as sight words. In doing this he uses a variety of word analysis skills which include phonics, word form clues, context clues and structural clues.

Speaking, writing and reading relationships are matured by the use of *experience reading charts* based on specific experiences and activities translated into written symbols. The teacher reads the charts for the class at first, but gradually some of the children are able to help. There are several forms of charts which are appropriate and are valuable in teaching language relationships. At least four types should be used:

1. *Personal language charts* which are a record of children's own language. These can be recorded on the chalkboard or on newsprint. They are to be highly perishable and never kept for other children to read. In fact, the child doing the dictating should never be required to read what he has said. Such a procedure causes a child to use only the words he can read, thus promoting language regression. One of the values of the personal language chart is its invitation to use *real language*. It should be enjoyed and then discarded or erased.

2. *Work charts* which are developed to give organization and guidance to classroom activities. These charts are of a more permanent nature. They should be developed with picture clues and other clues which will enable children to use them. Charts can be used for planning experiences as well as summarizing them. The planning chart helps establish the child's purpose and keeps "what we want to find out" in focus. Charts can include experiences developed by one group as "do-it-yourself" activities for others. An important thing to remember is that the charts should be developed *with* the children. They may be revised when children find that their ideas didn't work.

3. *Narrative charts* which might be records of shared experiences of the group. When a class group makes an excursion, cooks, has a visitor in the classroom or has a pet for a day or more, it can record the experiences on a number of charts. Charts can be used to summarize learnings from reference materials or reading on one topic from several books. These charts lend themselves to more repetition of certain words that are inherent in the discussion. They can be used for follow-up activities such as reading to each other, finding words that are alike, finding words that begin alike, etc.

# PERSONAL LANGUAGE CHARTS

Michael
Daddy bird is
bringing worms to
mother bird and the
little babies

My Three Dogs
by Andy

I have three dogs
and they are bassett
hounds. Their names
are Dudley, Aggie,
and Ozzie. They eat
dog food and sleep
in the kitchen. The
fattest dog is Dudley.
Ozzie is the thinnest.
Aggie is two years
old.

Easel painting with
dictated story.

Chalkboard story
dictated to teacher.

Lizards
by Mike
I have a lizard.
She is small.
She eats bugs.
She lays eggs.
She has two babies.
The babies are three
inches long.
I like them.

Stories and pictures made into a book.

This is a green worm.
It eats green tomato leaves.
It is fun to see.
It will be a moth.
            by Susan

This is a praying mantis.
I found it.
It is a good insect.
It eats bad insects.
            by Larry

# WORK CHARTS

## Helpers for Today

 Water plants

Bobby

 Feed fish

Nancy

 Clean playhouse

Tom
Betty

**Classroom activities**

## Our Trip to the Bird Farm
## What We Want to Know

1. Why don't the birds fly away?
2. Where do the birds come from?
3. How many kinds of birds are at the farm?
4. Which birds have to be kept in cages?

**Establishing purpose**

## Our Trip to the Bird Farm
## Getting Ready

1. Bring permission slips from home.
2. Bring a sack lunch.
3. Choose a partner for the bus ride.
4. Learn the safety rules

**Planning experiences**

## Our Trip to the Bird Farm
## Some Things We Learned

1. The toucan has a funny looking beak.
2. Flamingos bend their knees backward.
3. Ducks and geese migrate.
4. Parakeets make good pets.

**Summarizing experiences**

# WORK CHARTS

## Study Rules

1. Look and listen.
2. Follow instructions.
3. Do good work.
4. Check your work.

We have two new easels.

Now we can paint.

We take turns.

We try to be neat.

# WORK CHARTS

## We Have Helpers

| | | |
|---|---|---|
| Flag salute | ———— | Dora |
| Messenger | ———— | Aaron |
| Milk | ———— | David |
| Waste basket | ———— | Cathy |
| Line leaders | ———— | Gary |
| | | Linda |
| Hostess | ———— | Jean |
| Balls | ———— | Joe |

## We Want to Find Out

1. Does air weigh anything?
2. What makes the wind blow?
3. How far does air go in space?
4. Where does fog come from?
5. How is lightning formed?

# NARRATIVE CHARTS

## Gingerbread Boys

Each of us made
  a gingerbread boy.
They were brown.
They were good
  to eat.

A cooking experience.

## Wild Flowers

We went for a walk.
We looked for wild flowers.
We found many kinds.
They were many colors.
They were many shapes.

An excursion.

## Sandra's Cat

Sandra's cat came to school.
Her mother brought it.
It was hungry.
We fed it some milk.
It slept in a basket.
We liked the little white
  kitten.

A visit from a pet.

# NARRATIVE CHARTS

This is Snip.

He is a black and white
    kitten

He came to school to visit.

He was a good kitten.

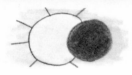

On Tuesday there was an eclipse.

We used a globe, a moon-ball,
    and flashlight to see how
    it would happen.

We saw pictures of it next day.

# READING SKILL CHARTS

## At the Beach

See the shells.
See the sand.
See the sailboats.
See the big ocean.

Repetition of words.
Words that begin alike.

## Family Words

 Mother  Baby

 Father

 Brother

 Sister

 Home

Words on a topic.

## Words We Know

| Color | Size | Smell | Sound | Space |
|-------|------|-------|-------|-------|
| red | little | sweet | quiet | astronaut |
| blue | big | stink | noise | missile |
| black | large | | | rocket |
| | tiny | | | planet |

Vocabulary charts to be expanded
by children.

56

# READING SKILL CHARTS

## Here Are Some Halloween Words

 ghost

 owl

 witch

 skeleton

 bat

 jack-o-lantern

black cat

Add     —s     —ed     —ing

| | |
|---|---|
| jumps | plays |
| jumped | played |
| jumping | playing |
| works | paints |
| worked | painted |
| working | painting |

4. *Reading skill charts* which are developed in the classroom for teaching and practice of some specific reading skill. In addition to practice in such fundamental skills as left-to-right eye movement and line-to-line progression, reading skill charts are effective for such skills as:

- Sounding out words as they are said and written down.

- Developing awareness of sentence structure.

- Emphasizing word structure when adding—*s, ed, ing,* etc.

- Using context clues to recognize a word that looks like another word.

Charts can be used for vocabulary development in a number of ways, one of which is to accumulate words specifically related to a particular unit or topic of study. They can also help in reading such things as numbers, dimensions, volume, sets, fractions.

When making the experience reading charts, there is opportunity for social development which is an important part of reading development. Children develop in their appreciation and consideration of the contributions of others. They also gain status in the group as their ideas and contributions are accepted and respected. This status is a factor which motivates children to undertake the writing of individual books and to continue to contribute their ideas to the class.

### Making and Reading Books

As the teacher works with reading material which has been produced in the classroom, there is increased interest in painting and dictating stories with a purpose. The teacher collects children's illustrated stories into class books for the library table. There can be a collection of stories on many topics or a collection on one topic. As children become productive enough, their individual stories, or an individual story, can be collected into a book. The teacher should provide the necessary materials and help in making attractive bindings. It is important that each child experiences *individual authorship* before the end of the kindergarten year or the first grade as the case may be and that he has repeated experiences in individual authorship throughout his school life.

Self-confidence in sharing one's ideas grows as children see the results of *their* accomplishments in a tangible form such as a book. They see the details of their work as meaningful parts of "something bigger." This experience develops a feeling about communication and the development of communication skills which cannot be built from doing worksheets for practice and correction. To do a paper "because the teacher says so" has little potential for building confidence in self-expression or in deepening appreciation for the ability of others to express their ideas through good writing.

The making of books suggests reasons for practicing basic language skills such as:

- Writing neatly and legibly.
- Organizing ideas in sequential patterns.
- Using accurate meanings.
- Using newly acquired words.
- Using clear, good sentence structure.
- Understanding that books are written to serve many purposes.

Books which are developed in the classroom must have equal status on the library table with those which are provided from the school library. The attitude of the teacher and her treatment of the children's books are important elements in developing an environment in which an individual will contribute to a class book or will author an individual book. In addition, the making of class books and individual books causes children to gain a deep appreciation for books which other people have written. The making of books by children is one of the stepping stones to a lifetime of enjoyment of reading.

## Developing Awareness of Common Vocabulary

From the beginning of recognizing words on dictated stories, children gain an awareness that some words seem to be used by everybody. It is through this interest that children begin to move from recognizing words in their own stories to recognizing words in stories of other children in the classroom, and eventually to recognizing the same words in books that are in their environment.

In the beginning experiences there should be no effort to control the use of specific words or to assure repetition of words. The abundance of language experiences assures needed repetition. In effect, it places "control" with each pupil. Mastery of the sight vocabulary comes at a later time in the school life of children. In the kindergarten and early first grade the responsibility of the teacher is to raise the level of awareness of pupils to the fact that our language contains many common words and patterns of expression. In the process some of the children may gain a sight vocabulary of basic words, but this development is not the goal for all children. It should always be a by-product of effective instruction and a good learning environment.

As children begin to demonstrate an awareness and a desire to be able to recognize words, incomplete sentences are useful in introducing into the classroom environment some of the words of highest frequency in the English language. They include a vocabulary that is much like that introduced in pre-primers, but they are characterized by an openness which requires that each child participate with his own ideas and his own language. Class books made with these sentences completed and their illustrations offer sufficient repetition of words to develop sight vocabularies of high frequency words without limiting the vocabulary to those words.

Incomplete sentences may be developed from a list of high frequency words in the English language such as the *Madden-Carlson* or the *Dolch List.* They may be formulated from a word list from a series of preprimers which will be made available for children to read.

Children are ready for these sentences soon after they have expressed an interest in writing on their own. Depending on the class, they may be introduced to the total class or to a small group within the class. Exposure to the activity has value for some children who do not participate in the writing. Suggested procedure might be:

1. Select an incomplete sentence which is appropriate for the class and teaching situation, for example: "I like to ____."

2. Engage the children in talking about things they like to do.

3. Write on the chalkboard in large letters, **"I like to** ____." Talk about the letters and how to form them as the writing is taking place. (Children should have had enough previous experience in observing dictation to know what writing is and to know the names of letters.)

4. Ask each child who is participating to make a crayon drawing of something he likes to do. Ask him to leave space at the bottom of the page for writing. He might fold his paper so he has a guide to his coloring space and his writing space.

5. After the picture is completed, the child copies the incomplete sentence from the chalkboard and asks the teacher for help on the word or words he needs to complete it. The teacher can write the necessary words on a strip of paper for the child to copy or write the word on the picture for children who may be having difficulty with copying.

6. The teacher collects ten or twelve pages for a book and makes a cover for it so that it may be used in small groups for

060452

reading. The idea of making a book rather than dealing with loose sheets of paper is very important.

7. The teacher may use the books for several days with various arrangements of children such as:

- The children who have their pages in a book will read together. Authors of pages can tell more about the pictures than the sentence tells.

- Children who did *not* write the sentences for a book can try to read it. They may be expected to read the high frequency words without being able to recognize the completion words. They may be able to read the completion words from picture clues.

- A child who is able to do so may read a whole book to the class.

- The books can be placed on the library table for all children to enjoy.

8. Words that are used in the incomplete sentences should be made part of the room environment so that all children can have them for ready reference when they are writing independently. The words may be strung on shoestrings to make "word ladders," they may be placed on a chart for a bulletin board or they may be placed on the chalkboard in a place that will not be erased.

9. After a few experiences in using incomplete sentences which are completely open-ended, the teacher may introduce initial consonants by asking children to complete sentences with at least one word which begins with a selected consonant. The writing should be preceded by a discussion of and identification of words which begin with the selected consonant.

- Examples: See my b————. I have a little f————.

    Look at the d————. This is a funny g——.

This exercise gives children a real experience in relating beginning sound to symbol. Rather than dealing with the same words over and over, they have to relate this skill to their own speaking experience.

10. Review the words which have been introduced in incomplete sentences with many kinds of games and activities. When a child does the oral composition for a story he is writing to accompany an easel painting, he should be helped to recognize words he will be using by referring to the word ladders or the bulletin board chart. Children can volunteer to "climb the ladder" by reading all the words from bottom to top. They can make up their own games which will give them review opportunities. The important thing is that these high frequency words become a part of the sight vocabulary and the spelling vocabulary with a minimum of analysis of the words. Exposure and frequency of use are more important at this stage of reading development than the refinement of word-analysis skills.

### Expanding Vocabulary

Children can listen to and enjoy stories that are read to them. In addition to the enjoyment, teachers can use the oral reading time to give positive illustrations of points that arise as children dictate their own stories. The teacher points out the variety of ways authors begin sentences, their use of more than one descriptive word at a time, the use of action words, and other aspects of good language likely to be duplicated in the oral speech of the children.

It is at the point when children are beginning to understand the concept that any word they can say can be written that they begin to use wide-range vocabulary in dictating, and subsequently in writing and reading. It is essential that children live in a classroom with wide-range vocabulary and experience the use of their "full language power" before they come under the influence of the highly controlled vocabularies of "readers." It is just as important that they continue to have the use of their full language power as they continue through school and use materials which are prepared with controlled vocabularies to teach specific reading skills.

Books that utilize the skills of alphabetizing can be made by children of all ages. Such books, when properly developed, interest children in increasing their useful vocabularies. The simplest ones are picture dictionaries, but the English language is growing so fast that older children can profit greatly from the development of Space Age dictionaries. All along the line, vocabulary development can be promoted by the development of books that challenge individuals or groups of children to organize words according to the order of the alphabet. Some variations of such an activity are:

1.  Finding in the story words beginning with as many letters of the alphabet as possible.

2.  Finding words which are used to introduce and conclude conversation and that begin with as many letters of the alphabet as possible.

3.  Finding words that describe "how big" and "how little" that begin with as many letters of the alphabet as possible.

4.  Making alphabet books with the use of name and action words from studies and discussions, as:

    *   *People We Know*
    *   *Animals*
    *   *Space*
    *   *Astronomy*
    *   *Mother's Work.*

Other kinds of word study booklets should be kept in the classroom at all times for vocabulary development. This can be done by developing bulletin boards to which children make contributions before they are bound into a study book, or by placing blank books in the room with titles that suggest different kinds of word study. Examples of titles are:

- *Things That are Round*
- *What I Discovered Today*
- *All Around Our Neighborhood*
- *Funny Things.*

Children can look through readers and other books and materials to find appropriate words to use in making a book in which each page has a word category for study. Words can be selected from their own stories or from other sources. They can do such activities as collecting:

- Words that end in *"ing."*
- Words that can be made longer.
- Contractions.
- English words for which they know the Spanish, French, or other foreign language equivalents.

**Writing Independently**

A desirable balance in communication skills cannot be developed or maintained unless children are able to write as well as to listen, talk, and read. Simple beginnings of writing in the early part of first grade need to be made concurrently with the development of word-recognition skills. By the same token, older children should engage regularly in writing their own ideas at the same time that they are reading what other people have written.

Early commitment to independent writing and reading is a major breakthrough for each child, not only in communication, but in other curriculum areas. The attitude of the learner which is required for a self-commitment to become productive in written expression is a most significant factor in developing long-range interest in improving quality of writing and in evolving a deep appreciation for well written literature.

A procedure that has been used successfully for making the paintings of children a springboard for writing—both dictation and independent writing—is:

1.  Not more than four colors need to be provided for any one day. If the teacher places four containers with a brush in each container on the floor, four children can paint at a time. This might be in addition to the children who paint at easels. The painting should be free from directions as far as ideas are concerned. The total range of ideas is being sought here.

2.  Some place in the classroom is designated as the place for a child to put his completed picture if he has a story about it to tell to the class. Each morning the teacher holds up the pictures (one at a time) and asks each artist to tell the class about his picture. During the "telling" she extracts two or three sentences that will describe the story and scribbles them on the back of the picture. In the afternoon she copies the

story on a story strip which can be pasted to the bottom of the picture.

3. The next day she shares the stories (in written form) with the children before she asks for new stories. In most classrooms the teacher can expect five or six paintings per day to be submitted for stories.

4. The paintings and stories can be placed in the classroom so that they can be "read" and used as reference for words in the future. A good way to do this is to use one side of an easel by running two bolts (five or six inches long) through the easel from the back. As each story is completed, holes are punched and it is threaded on the bolts. A thin strip of wood with holes punched to correspond with the bolts is then put on and all is secured with wing nuts. Stories can be added by removing the nuts and wood strip, threading on the stories, and replacing the nuts and wood strip.

5. Children are encouraged to read the stories and later to use them as a source of words when writing on their own.

6. The teacher continues to do the writing as long as necessary. Before long a child will ask to write on his own. This is a time the teacher has been waiting for. It is the "self-commitment" of one child, then another, and another that leads to individual writing and rapid progress in reading.

7.  The child who wants to write on his own is asked to tell the class what he thinks he will write. The teacher offers help in spelling words that the author is not sure about. This kind of individual help before the total class increases the awareness in all children of the skills necessary for independent work.

8.  As children write on their own, they need to be directed to the many resources in a classroom which offer help, such as labels, bulletin boards, stories in their books, word lists of high frequency words, story books, etc.

9.  A child will be able to read what he writes if it is truly independent writing. He is also ready to begin reading what other people have written. After three or four children have made a self-commitment, the teacher should begin the use of incomplete sentences.

10.  The next step is to place in the classroom books that are easy to read, including several copies of preprimers. Before long a child will discover that he can read most of one of these

books and will ask for help. From this point on, there develops in the classroom an emphasis on reading what other people have written as well as reading what is written in the classroom.

When children learn to read through experience, the pre-primers are not used to teach them how to read. If they are used, they should always be discovered by the children and used to give the teacher some clues as to how well they are learning how to read material which emphasizes the repetition of high frequency words. A child should be able to select from several preprimers. If he cannot read through a book orally in two or three sessions with the teacher, he is not ready for this kind of reading.

# THE READING DEVELOPMENT SCHEDULE

Children who learn to read through experience should have opportunities for contact with the following language experiences during the kindergarten-primary years. The position of the lines indicates the general order of introducing them in relation to other language experiences. This presents a developmental pattern which children will follow, in general, but does not, since it cannot, indicate when any one child will move into the next stage.

| ACTIVITY | SCHOOL ENTRANCE | TO | END OF PRIMARY |
|---|---|---|---|
| 1. Sharing ............... | | daily by some children mostly oral | |
| 2. Discussing (planned) .... | | at least once a week around a selected theme | |
| 3. Listening to stories ........ | | daily | |
| 4. Telling stories ............... | | by teacher occasionally group activity at least once a week | |
| 5. Dictating ............... | | to teacher | by teacher |

| ACTIVITY | SCHOOL ENTRANCE | TO | END OF PRIMARY |
|---|---|---|---|
| 6. Developing speaking, .... writing, reading relationships | | informal, as teaching opportunities arise | |
| | | planned program of word recognition skills | |
| 7. Making books ............ | | class books as they are produced — individual books | |
| | | at least two per semester | |
| 8. Developing awareness .. of common vocabulary | | informal, as teaching opportunities arise | |
| | | emphasis on 250 words of highest frequency | |
| 9. Expanding vocabulary .. | | painting and writing with full-range vocabulary encouraged | |
| | | individual writing handbooks which promote vocabulary growth | |

| ACTIVITY | SCHOOL ENTRANCE | TO | END OF PRIMARY |
|---|---|---|---|
| 10. Writing independently .. | | with "starter" phrases and words ———————→ | |
| | | | with "starter" ideas |
| 11. Reading whole books .... | | reading with teacher, books selected cooperatively | |
| | | reading with teacher from self-selected book ←— | |
| 12. Improving style and ...... form | ——listening and observing oral reading | | |
| | | seminars and critiques on style and form at least once a week | |
| 13. Using a variety of ........ resources | | establish a writing center as children engage in independent writing | |
| | | establish a reference reading center for special studies in science and —— social studies | |

| ACTIVITY | SCHOOL ENTRANCE | TO | END OF PRIMARY |
|---|---|---|---|
| 14. Reading a variety of symbols | informal, as teaching opportunities arise ——→ | | select one kind of *special reading* skill to discuss ——→ and develop once per month ——→ |
| 15. Studying words | group oral work in helping children understand relationship between sounds in oral language and their symbols in written language —— from oral composition | from words selected for specific study ←— - - - from written composition ——→ | |
| 16. Improving comprehension | | weekly checks with individual children on simple comprehension skills ——→ pupil-kept records of reading skills recommended ——→ | |

KEY: — — — indicates incidental learning
———— indicates planned program

73

# 4

# A GOOD LEARNING ENVIRONMENT

## THE PHYSICAL ENVIRONMENT

An inviting, exciting and comfortable room in which to live increases children's enthusiasm for learning tremendously. Such an environment can be accomplished in a variety of ways.

### The Classroom

Let us first think about the classroom itself apart from the personal activities and relationships of the teacher and the group. It needs to appear as light and gay as possible. There should be the effect of spaciousness which may need to be created in small rooms by judicious arrangement of furniture. It is better, for instance to have open areas and fewer and narrower pathways between groups of tables than wide pathways and no space.

Why is this space needed? First, it gives psychological breathing space for both teacher and children. Second, it provides areas for children to congregate in groups, either formal or informal, for many of the varied acivities which take place all day long.

The room should seem restful in its overall effect but should have areas of exciting contrasts and gay color. The myriad ways in which this can be done inexpensively with paper or paint are limited only by the ingenuity of the teacher or her ability to stimulate ideas in children.

The room should be neat and show the results of good community housekeeping. This does not mean that things should be so put away that children can not live in the room comfortably, but there do need to be some clear spaces for all sorts of temporary use. In fact a room may be "orderly" even though it is "jam-packed" with things that children need and are constantly using, if these things are well arranged and well cared for.

So much for the room itself. Now comes the problem of creating in it a stimulating environment—one which will arouse children's enthusiasm for learning.

**The world of nature**

One of the major objectives of education is to help children understand better the world around them. Anything from the real world in which children are or can become interested and which reasonably can be brought into the school room has a rightful place there. Fish, birds, other animals, plants and flowers both for beauty and other purposes, rocks and minerals and what ever else will stimulate curiosity, questions and understanding.

The teacher's responsibility is to start such a collection and then inspire children so they will see things which they find interesting and which they wish to share with their friends. As children take responsibility for bringing in additions to the room collections, they confirm their own interest as well as extend their own understanding and development. These collections can be used for various purposes as will be discussed later.

**Books, records, pictures**

Next in value to first hand contact with nature are our secondary sources. These give us recorded information but,

even more important, others' interpretation of that information. They add great wealth to the classroom and their selection should be guided by worthiness and variety. Thoughtful selection will add to children's enjoyment of them and at the same time make possible children's evaluation of such resources.

That all secondary sources are someone's interpretation is an extremely important concept for children to understand. It should lead to their right to question, their need for information with which to evaluate, their acceptance of differing points of view and the right of each individual to his own reactions and feelings. This in turn can lead to increased confidence in one's own thinking which he knows will be evaluated in turn by others but which he still has the right to express.

More specifically, books need to be of a wide range of difficulty, of subjects, and of types. There should be picture books for all levels, story books, books for information and for reference, prose and poetry, serious books and humorous books.

Records should be for listening, for singing, for dancing, for learning, for background music while working and for relaxing. They should include vocal and instrumental music, stories and poems, information and directions. Except perhaps for some borrowed or precious records, children should always be able to play the records themselves. It is helpful if the record player has a tone control so that the music may be kept soft when a group is enjoying listening while others are working.

Pictures also need to be of many kinds and for a variety of uses. Large pictures to be hung on the wall need to be changed frequently or they become unnoticed. They must be of fine quality and a variety of styles and types as children gain much of their early appreciation of art from them.

Pictures on the bulletin boards can stimulate questions and interest in whatever area the teacher feels these children need to explore. Mounted pictures for children's handling can be excellent sources of information relating to innumerable problems, also stimulating interest and curiosity.

### Equipment and supplies

Much of the equipment and supplies is fairly routine such as paper, scissors, pastes, colored chalk, paints, brushes and crayons. Most classrooms have tables and chairs, easels and chart racks. Many are now including individual film strip viewers, radios and record players or listening posts for tapes and records. In some cases animal cages, and basic materials for an aquarium or terrarium are available. If choices must be made there are some criteria. Other things being equal it is more important to have equipment which starts with and extends and diversifies children's existing interests than that which carries out the teacher's interest. Better development results from complete and thorough use of a few pieces than from sketchy uncertain use of many. In general equipment should be such that the children themselves can use it. This is particularly true of the record player, slide projector, radio, animal cages and bottles and jars for all sorts of specimens, alive or not, brought in by the children.

Children should be taught *how* and *when* to handle equipment and materials rather than not to handle them. It is an unnecessary frustration and the loss of an excellent learning situation to bring interesting objects into the classroom only to say, "Don't touch."

The implication of this for supplies in general is important, too. Paper should be easily and readily available to children. So should the paints and crayons and scissors. Initial discussions of how and when they should be used, where children are assisted with the process of thinking about the problems involved, can result in children making their own decisions. When problems arise children should re-examine these decisions and modify them as they see necessary. This develops responsibility and self-direction and frees the teacher for much more appropriate and constructive activity.

## TEACHER-PUPIL RELATIONSHIPS

The quality and characteristics of the teacher-pupil interaction is without doubt the most important single factor in the child's learning. An important part of this relationship depends on the teacher's ability to provide real leadership and guidance which maintains needed controls at the same time it develops each child's ability to direct and control himself. It order to do this children must first and foremost see *the teacher as a friend*. This does not mean that she lets them do whatever they want.

But rather she is there to help them, she is on their side and they can trust her. She will not put them in defeating or untenable positions. She will not betray them nor make them look ridiculous. They can count on her to respect each of them as a person.

### The teacher establishes limits with children

This should not and cannot be done "once and for all" at the beginning of the year. Lists of rules of what we will and will not do, no matter how developed, are, first, not very effective and, second, subtly suggestive of undesirable behavior. They often bring to children's attention actions which otherwise would never have occurred to them, at least at the moment. Better procedure is to help children recognize problems as they arise and plan to solve them. Also, when embarking on a new activity, planning with children as to how to carry it out most effectively prevents many problems from occurring. This is quite different in procedure and in effect from setting up general rules in advance of need, and which children are expected to apply to new situations which they may not see as related.

Rather as any type of problem arises, the teacher may stop the particular activity and say that this is not working very well. She may then ask children what they think the problem is and how they think they might work it out better. In doing this it is important that the teacher *handle the discussion in such a way that children feel free to express their own personal reactions rather than what they think the teacher wants them to say.* This is more difficult than it might seem especially where the children see the teacher as the "authority," the giver and expecter of "right" answers. It is not as difficult where the teacher does not evaluate each suggestion but only accepts it for consideration by the group. If an already indoctrinated child says, "That is not right," or "That is not the way," the teacher may counter with the idea that there are a number of ways, maybe some better than any of us have yet thought of.

### The teacher may raise questions or problems which the children do not see

This is an ever available means for adult leadership and guidance. From experience teachers are aware of factors and problems which do not occur to children. If these are likely to make a real difference it is the teacher's responsibility to bring them to the attention of the group. If they then do not want to modify their plans on the basis of them they should be allowed to procede, providing, of course, the results will not be too serious. We must protect children's health and well being, but experiencing the effect of factors whose impact they are unable to gauge is the only sound basis for real understanding which they can then use in future self-direction.

This discussion does not mean to imply that the teacher is not in control of the group at all times. But to the extent that this control can be exercised by the children with understanding and purpose, to that extent is learning improved. Not only is the amount of learning increased but the quality of it as well. The learning that is achieved in reading, for instance, is more related to the essence of what reading really is, and becomes more available to children in their further learning.

### The teacher maintains limits already established with children

There are many reasons why children do not always act within established limits. They desirably become engrossed in their own pursuits of individual goals and do not realize they are transgressing. They may not recognize what they are doing as going beyond the limits they helped establish. The obvious procedure here is for the teacher to help children see their behavior in relation to the limits they have accepted.

In the small percentage of situations where "breaking the rules" is conscious and intentional it is of prime importance for the teacher to understand why the child needs to do this. The importance increases in proportion to the extent and frequency that the child's hostility is expressed. Compliance may be required of the child at the moment if the transgression is serious, but the first order of business at the first opportunity becomes one of understanding how to reduce the child's need for rebelling.

The importance of this step may be seen when we realize that learning is a main goal accepted by the teacher and the group. A child who needs to rebel can do it most successfully and effectively by refusing to learn. We might force a child to stay in his chair but we cannot force him to learn. He does this only because he wants to. Many children who are capable of excellent learning are seen by the school as unable to learn because they subconsciously express their hostilities by not learning. Anything in the situation which increases this hostility makes them that much less able to learn. It is of supreme importance to develop the ability to establish and maintain needed controls in such a way that children have freedom needed for learning.

### The teacher establishes freedom for various purposes

The teacher needs to be able to see children in enough free situations so that she can make the kind of observations that help her understand each child's developmental progress and needs. If the child is always in a strictly controlled situation (which is needed for some activities) the teacher cannot find out how he is developing his own controls or self-direction, nor discover his interests and concerns.

The child needs freedom to seek out and carry on experiences and activities which he needs for his own development. Since each individual's developmental needs are different it is impossible to meet them all by directed activity. In addition, some of these needs, notably the need for developing self-direction, can only by met in a relatively free and undirected

*Department of Education, San Diego County, California*

situation. The over control, and over direction, of most children in today's classrooms is at least a major factor in many of the serious problems which show up later both in emotional maturity and school learning.

One such problem is the lack of interest in school work and resistance to it. Where "school work" is always seen as "something I'm supposed to do because the teacher wants me to," there is often little real incentive to accomplish it. Further, not doing it becomes a most satisfactory means of exercising power against the teacher and expressing hostilities toward her.

Another result which may well be even more serious is that the child never learns to direct his own learning or be independent in his own study procedures. This deplorable situation is found from elementary school on through graduate school.

In these days when we are so aware that learning must be continuous throughout the life of each of us, the lack of the ability or desire to direct one's own learning becomes a very serious matter. Since individuals learn only through their own experiences, self-directed learning must be encouraged and made *satisfying* from the earliest school years on.

Another kind of freedom which teachers can establish is freedom to make mistakes, to be wrong. Children can be so controlled that each error is also a transgression against authority and therefore "bad." If instead mistakes are accepted as natural and used as the stuff of which learning is made, much is gained. There is a drop in guilt feelings and a tremendous gain in learning how to recognize errors and use them on their own to obtain correct solutions.

Still another freedom is that of doing something different from what others are doing because it meets present needs. Continuously controlled and directed learning where each in the class, or at least in the group, is doing the same thing at the same time makes children unable to accept doing something different. They cannot face reading out of a different book or learning different words or doing different arithmetic activities which they may need desperately because it singles them out as different. Where each child has freedom to do something different from what others are doing a good share of the time, this does not become an issue.

## A kindred relationship between teachers and pupils is flexibility

Here teachers accept and encourage different ways of accomplishing group-established goals. This eliminates much of the "this-is-the-way" type of direction. Instead it challenges children to figure out other better ways of accomplishing goals which they have decided on or at least accepted. Evaluation, individual and group, can help children see there are many ways, some better than others, but still room for individuality. It is this type of relationship which is essential for the development of creativity and of independent and critical thinking as well as effective self-direction.

### The teacher develops the child's ability to make wise decisions

When we realize each individual will or should be making his own decisions about many things all his life, we can see the importance of developing ability to do this. It has been said the whole purpose of education is to enable people to make better decisions. It is obvious the effect this has in turn upon better learning. One means of doing this is to set up a situation or use an existing one to *help children recognize and identify the problem that needs solution.* For example, a group of children had been miscalling several words so that it prevented their understanding of the passages read. They felt they needed to learn more words before they read these stories. Since they realized they were not getting the meaning the teacher raised the question of whether they could get the meaning by another approach. Here was a word they did not know. Could they make a reasonable guess as to the meaning of the sentence without knowing that word? They went back and put the thread of the story in their own words, then read the sentence leaving out the unknown word. Nearly all of them said, "Oh, that must be ————." The teacher then asked if that looked reasonable and they brought out various other means of word identification and since they all checked out, decided they had figured out the word for themselves. So they realized that it wasn't isolated word study they needed but a better command of the use of context clues. A better decision had been made.

If children are going to learn to make decisions it is obvious there are going to have to be decisions for them to make. While for each of us there are some decisions we do not have the privilege of making, recognizing the choices in which we do have freedom is extremely important. Children early need to be made aware of these. When goals are arrived at and agreed upon, then there are nearly always a variety of ways to work toward the goal be it specific or general. Too often we do not recognize alternatives nor even explore for them. We operate on a "this-is-the-way" basis derived probably from our limited experience. Children with more limited experience may do this even more. When we are willing to believe there is always a better way if we can find it, we can set up situations so this can happen. We can say to children, "You need to learn to understand better how the people in the story are feeling and why they do what they do. Now, it might help if you thought about it as you are reading, or if you pretend you are one of these people or maybe you will think of a way that is still better for you." Or it may be as simple as saying, "We have decided you have these things to do. You decide which you think it would be best to do first."

When we are helping children make choices we need to help them consider bases for decision. What kind of questions do we need to ask? What factors need to be considered? What values do we use when we decide that one basis is more important than another?

This can be explored in the process of establishing procedures for choosing their own books. They need to consider whether the book looks interesting, whether or not they are able to read it, if it meets some specific need of theirs at the time. If they decide there is nothing about the book that makes them want to read it or see any value in reading it, this is probably sufficient basis for decision, at least until they can and do come to see some value in it. The consideration of how easy or difficult a book will be for them to read is influenced largely by why they want to read it, what its value is to them. Just reading lots of books may be a very real value to a child for a time and should be honored while other values are developing. A "too difficult" book may present a challenge or provide needed information or increase a child's confidence in his reading ability and hence in himself. Then, no matter what the areas or situation, having given children choices we must honor them, and then help them decide afterwards if their choice was wise or how they think they might do it now.

### The teacher needs to stimulate initiative and self-direction and build self-confidence in children

Her success in accomplishing this makes more difference in children's learning than perhaps everything else she does put together. And it takes no time away from her teaching for it results from the *way* in which she works with the children rather than from "something else that must be taught." There are a number of procedures which make a difference.

*A positive approach.* As the teacher comments on what the child has done which is desirable, he becomes aware himself of what he has done and can do which is good and which has brought him success and recognition. Eliminating the negative as far as possible by ignoring mistakes and undesirable behavior helps to eliminate these by not calling the child's attention to them. *This does not mean we do nothing about them.* Rather we use the situation for positive teaching.

For instance, when a child makes an error in reading, we do not point out the error but call his attention to the word or phrase in a different setting which provides enough guidance to insure his success. He then is able to return to the first situation successfully, although this may not be either necessary or desirable. He may rather go on to another new situation where he may have further success. This procedure also applies to errors in behavior.

*Help children recognize and focus on successes rather than failures.* So often we seem to concentrate on what children *cannot* do rather than on what they can. We say, "That is wrong," when actually it is right except for one word, letter, number or behavior. If instead we say, "That is almost right," or "That is all right but one," the child's feeling about himself and his ability is vastly different. Spelling is a good example of where children are told a word is wrong when it maybe right except for one letter missing, added or exchanged.

*Recognize and encourage initiative.* It is a sad commentary that schools on the one hand complain about the lack of initiative and responsibility of children, on the other they reprimand the child who exhibits these qualities for not following directions or doing what he is "supposed to." We control so much of a child's day that the only possible way he can exert initiative is to break through routines and controls. When children do this we need to look at what it is the child is doing and why. He may need to develop better judgment but let's not kill his initiative in the process.

Far better it is to do everything we can to develop this initiative even though it may be somewhat disrespectful of our well laid and smoothly operating plans. The ability to use initiative and accept responsibility needs to be developed early if it is ever to be really effective.

*Set up situations to stimulate self-confidence and self-direction.* Using the regular classroom activities to accomplish these purposes is a first step which under some situations may be quite limited. To extend these characteristics of children it becomes necessary to organize and carry out learning situations and expectancies with this in mind. Self-confidence can not develop where more is often expected of a child than he can perform. The youngster who is always just holding on by his finger tips is bound to be anxious about his ability to continue to hold on. He must feel sure, solid ground under his feet. This necessarily means modifying both what we expect of him and what he expects of himself. This means providing different reading material with which he can feel or develop confidence. Sometimes children in choosing their own material will stay at an "easy" level so long we fear they will make no progress. It may be that this is confidence-building time and when they feel themselves on solid ground they may make rapid progress. It

may be that we can encourage this by our positive approach and expression of confidence. Seldom if ever should this be forced; too early testing may crumble the newly developing confidence.

As children get really involved and take off under their own steam they notoriously accomplish more than they could or would under constant teacher direction. As we listen to ourselves we become aware of the extent to which we direct the actions and behavior of the children in our classroom. We have many examples of children's ability to direct their own behavior and their own learning given the opportunity, a rich environment and reasonable guidance. Such children learn more and are forming the basis for much greater future learnings. It may be hard to accept but over direction of children can easily result in limiting rather than extending their progress.

## SETTING TASKS

Setting tasks or helping children set their own is a major function of teaching. For either of these purposes teachers must plan. In fact, preparation for planning *with* children may be more demanding than simply planning *for* children. The needs of each child must be recognized in either case and, recognizing that alternative plans should always be considered, preparation is an absolute essential for planning with children.

### Planning the lesson

Lesson planning is essential to good teaching. Inexperienced teachers need to write out their plans for each lesson each day in as much detail as they find helpful. More experienced teachers may do this mentally but in the absence of a specific procedure for lesson planning and the presence of many demands on time, this highly important task may be sadly neglected.

*Specific purpose.* The first requisite is to decide on the specific purpose for the lesson. To improve comprehension or increase word analysis skills is quite inadequate for a purpose. Where are these children in their skills of comprehension? Which of the numerous comprehension skills do they need right now? Which of the many word identification skills do they need? And what step in this skill are they ready for next? A reasonable specific purpose might read like this: Help these children sense the various factors in the story so that they are able to evaluate the behavior of the various characters and suggest and evaluate alternatives. Watch particularly to see if children are noting verb endings *s* and *ed*.

*Skills of learning.* The next step which determines how we teach the lesson, at least in part, is deciding which of the learning skills which these children need will contribute most to developing the lesson. Because of the rapid developments and changes which are taking place at an increasing rate in our society, every one of us needs to learn continuously for the rest of our lives. This will be increasingly so for the children we are teaching today and tomorrow. Thus one of our most important responsibilities to these children is to develop their skills of learning so that they may use them consciously and independently and get satisfaction from doing so.

There are innumerable learning skills but the most important of them may be included in communication skills, problem-solving skills, evaluative skills, self-direction skills and those of effective human relations. Again, these skills are not something else to be taught but only a better way of teaching what we will teach anyway. The major purpose of this volume is to help develop real communication skills as opposed to the mechanical skills often called "reading," "writing," "speaking" and "listening" where the form rather than the essence of each is taught, usually each in isolation from the other three. Real communication skills have been discussed throughout the book but mainly in Chapter 3. They may be summarized as:

- To understand what another means and express oneself so that others understand our meaning in both oral and written form.
- To interpret happenings, ideas and feelings.
- To identify with persons or situations in written or oral communication.
- To use others' communication so that one may predict on the basis of it.

Problem-solving skills which need to be developed so they may be used in all areas of learning may include:

- To observe accurately.
- To recognize and define a problem.
- To seek causes.

- To see relationships.

- To establish hypotheses and evaluate them.

- To withhold judgment.

- To generalize.

- To draw inferences and see implications.

- To develop alternatives and evaluate them.

- To draw defensible conclusions.

There are a number of research skills which children of all ages need, such as:

- To locate information.

- To evaluate resources.

- To skim to find desired material.

- To read for answers to questions they have asked.

Some of the human relationship skills which can be developed are:

- To work cooperatively with peers.

- To exercise leadership and membership skills.

- To show respect for each individual.

Skills of independence which all children need to learn and develop effectively include:

- To be self-directive toward realistic goals.

- To take initiative.

- To accept responsibility.

- To evaluate their own procedures for learning.

- To know when they know.

Coming back to the specific purpose of the lesson plan under discussion, "evaluation of alternatives" is a natural choice as a skill of learning to be further developed as a means of carrying out the purpose.

*Child's purpose.* The third step is looking at the lesson, the purpose stated, and, by thinking about the children involved, deciding how they can best become involved in the lesson, understand and identify with the purposes and in general come to consciously recognize and want to accomplish the purposes of the lesson.

*Content and procedures.* This step involves following through the previous steps in terms of the specific content and material to be used. It might be said here that at times some adjustment will need to be made at this point. We may recognize that the material we intended to use does not lend itself to our purposes and so we need to choose other material. Or if this is not possible we must change our purposes to those which can be accomplished with the present material. In this case we must always be sure that the new purposes are really defensible for *these* children at *this* time.

Other criteria we need to consider when setting up procedures for a lesson are: first, do they follow from what we know about how children learn; second, are they suited to the needs and abilities of these children; and third, do they provide variety, make use of background experience and involve other factors which will develop and maintain children's interest?

*Materials.* This last factor can make or break the success of the lesson. We plan certain activities, illustrations or demonstrations. If we neglect to prepare, select or collect the equipment, lists, objects or other materials we will need, thinking perhaps we can produce them or find them at the appropriate moment, all our planning may go for naught if we cannot locate them.

A lesson plan for developing a word identification skill might be somewhat as follows:

## LESSON PLAN FOR FIRST GRADE READING

### Group

Five children who in the last few days have shown lack of ability to use context clues in identifying new words.

### Specific Purpose

Help these children to know better how to go about using context clues.

### Skill of Learning

Help children make inferences and check them. They will decide what a word may be from sentence and story meaning.

### Establishing Children's Purpose

"When people read interesting books they often find words which they do not know. I do and each of you do when you read. There are a number of ways of finding out what these words are. A good way to try first is to figure out what the word might be from the rest of the sentence. Let's see if we can figure out some words we don't know."

### Procedure

Set up the chosen story for meaningful reading. Ask whomever first finds a word he does not know to raise his hand. Children read silently until one child raises his hand. They are warned, if any of them know the word, not to tell it. The child shows where the word is, three do not know it. Ask child to read the whole sentence aloud leaving out the unknown word. All others listen for sentence meaning with books closed.

The three are asked to think what the word might be, what word would make sense. If someone suggests a word which makes sense in the sentence, ask if it fits into the story. If so, then check it phonetically. Does the guessed word begin with the sound of the unknown word, end with the sound of it, have the same sound in the middle? See if the two who know the word agree. All read on silently till they find another word one or more do not know.

**Materials**

Five copies of any book which is at about or slightly above free-reading level for these children.

### DIAGNOSTIC TEACHING

The advancing field of child development has helped us to recognize that maximum learning comes from continuous progress for each child. The situation must be such that he may start where he is and move ahead as far and as fast as he is reasonably able. We also know that children vary greatly in their ability to make progress. One, there is great variation between children; two, children can usually learn faster in one area than in another; and three, each may be able to accomplish school learnings faster at one time than another depending on other factors.

These differences in children mean that fixed grouping by level of achievement is of little value and introduces questionable procedures as well. We are realizing that this is true within the classroom as well as among classrooms. Continuous progress at the optimum rate for individual children can never be obtained where children are put in stable groups where all are taught the same thing at the same time. The best answer seems to be diagnostic teaching.

Diagnostic teaching is the process of discovering and keeping track of each child's progress so that each day he may learn what he needs and is ready to learn. This results in maximum learning for him. Not only does this occur for the obvious reasons, but, because most of his efforts at learning are successful, he gains confidence in his ability to learn. This is perhaps the single most potent factor in his continuing success.

### How Can Diagnostic Teaching Be Done?

It is indicated in point 1 of planning the lesson that the specific purpose and materials should be derived from the immediate needs of the children. In order to plan effectively the teacher must determine what each child knows, and needs to know next, to provide a basis for deciding which specifics to teach next. This does not mean giving a test, at least not often. It does mean keeping for each child a continuous record of specific needs based on regular classroom behavior. This may be done as the teacher is working with the child individually or in a small group. In it are noted errors, failures, and also successes in areas of new learning for the child. From it can be pinpointed the child's needs for the immediate future.

As the teacher during planning time checks over these records for the class, the groups needed for the following day become evident. Next learnings can be planned in light of the skills of comprehension and independent word identification as discussed in Chapter 3. By eliminating our preconceived ideas and standardized routine procedure we can plan for children so they will no longer be "taught" what they already know or what they are not yet ready for. Since diagnostic teaching can be many times more effective, teachers can spend a much larger proportion of their time pinpointing children's needs.

*Grouping.* We have seen above what diagnostic teaching means for grouping. It means that children may be grouped according to current needs for the day or the week or as long as they have the same specific needs. More likely all grouping will not be the same for any two days though some may continue over a period of time. It means we will be teaching groups who really need the same learning at the same time, but only

*Department of Instructional Materials, Portland, Oregon Public Schools*

as long as this is so. It means that in many of the groups there will be a wide range in level of reading but that each child is having difficulty with the same specific comprehension skill, word identification skill or some other skill related to progress in reading.

Here is one answer to how a teacher has time to accomplish diagnostic teaching. A large portion of every school day is wasted both for the teacher and children when children are "taught" what they do not need or cannot learn. As this is eliminated, there is adequate time for evaluative teaching, which also provides an ideal situation for developing self-direction, responsibility, and self-evaluation.

There will also be another type of grouping, the friendship groups. These will be made up of those children who enjoy reading together or to each other. These, too, will change personnel frequently according to the children's wishes. Much of the time children will not be working in groups but rather reading a book they have selected for themselves. They may read as far and as fast as they wish within the time available to them. These books may be library books, basic or supplementary texts in reading or in any of the curriculum areas, or books which children bring from home.

*Reading a story together.* For any one of a number of reasons a group of children may be reading a story together and it is well to consider procedures based on what we know. First, since a group will all be reading it, there must be a specific purpose or they would not be doing it. Hence, this purpose needs to be established with them in advance. Second, each child then will read the story silently, probably at his seat, keeping in mind the purposes for which he is reading and doing whatever is necessary to carry them out.

Next they come together to discuss the story and whatever it was they were reading it for, sharing their interpretations. They do *not* read the story orally except in very rare instances. There are several reasons for this. There is no defensible purpose for reading it aloud. It is not a good way to develop oral reading skills. Since the others have all read it and thought about it, they have no particular interest in listening to it. Hence we would be undercutting our teaching of listening. We teach children not to listen by providing a situation where their listening is minimal. Oral reading is one of the poorest ways of telling whether or not children have understood the story. Getting them to talking about the story is much more effective. Hence it becomes a relatively useless activity, one in which children are not particularly interested and one with which they can become bored, as is evidenced by the frequent lack of attention. Children may be interested in reading orally themselves but very seldom in listening to others read something they have already read. The practice of oral reading then tends to decrease rather than increase children's interest in reading. Instead the time can better be spent in helping children develop one or more of their comprehension skills, their learning skills and, if different, their specific purposes for reading this story together.

*Oral and silent reading.* By far the greatest amount of reading individuals will do, in school as well as out, is silent. It is in silent reading that all the major comprehension skills need to be developed. Also silent reading is much easier, even from the beginning, than is oral reading which requires all the skills of silent reading plus those of oral interpretation. Saying single words out loud as children recognize them is *not* oral reading and children should never come to believe it is.

A child should never be asked to read anything orally which he has not read silently, except in a testing situation alone with the teacher. We can get away from the struggling-separate-word-saying process if from the first stages of book reading we ask children to look at the next line, read it to themselves, then tell us what it says. This way the child can work out any problems, ask for help if needed and then say the entire sentence with meaning. If he cannot do this, then he is not ready to read this material. Only after the story has been read and discussed for meaning may it be used for reinforcing vocabulary development and word identification skills.

*Developing oral reading skills.* The major purpose for oral reading is to share with someone else something which they do not know but would like to hear. It needs a truly audience situation. A situation for good teaching then requires the following: 1) the selection to be read aloud must not have been read by most of those listening; 2) it should be chosen by the reader as something he can, with practice, read well; 3) he should decide on a selection which he believes his listeners will like to hear; 4) he must thoroughly prepare the selection so that he can read it effectively.

By developing oral reading through these procedures, any child can share with a group, large or small, something he has found of interest. The selection by the child of what he wants to share and feels he can, with preparation, read effectively insures this. By selecting material new to the rest of the children he will have an interested audience which also contributes to his successful experience. The preparation and success insure his development of these skills so that by having such an experience once or twice a month more progress is made than by his daily taking his turn reading a portion of the story all have been working on. Group evaluation, where improvements and "what-we-especially-like-about-it" comments constitute the bulk of the discussion, sets goals and stimulates desires for progress. With the group thus freed of the time-consuming "reading around the circle" more time is available for developing the all important comprehension skills.

*Developing comprehension skills.* Discussion is an excellent way to develop comprehension skills but it must be planned specifically for this purpose. Questions or statements calculated to get children to tell what the book *says,* should be minimum. These are valuable sometimes for introducing the discussion or as a means of clarifying misconceptions or differences of opinion. They should represent only a small portion of the discussion.

The main emphasis should be on what the sentence, paragraph, story *means.* Can the children visualize and identify with the situation, the characters, their purposes and behaviors? Can they see alternative behaviors and evaluate them in relation to the behaviors in the story? Can they project beyond the situation? Predict what might happen next? Can they interpret and identify with the feelings of the characters? Can they draw implications from the material read? Can they get a clear, concise understanding of the meaning of the material.

In the books read early the concepts are usually simple and clear. Children can learn to get meaning in all the ways mentioned above quite easily. As the material grows more complex, the comprehension skills need to be continued rigorously so they become mental habits with all reading. All are not always appropriate to every selection but during each week each child needs to develop most of his comprehension skills further.

## EVALUATION

Evaluation is a key ingredient in any and all teaching. Too often it is inadequately carried out because of misunderstanding of its real meaning. Evaluation and marking or grading are two completely separate procedures. Evaluation should be continuous, grading at intervals. Evaluation is specific, grading general. Evaluation helps to analyze needs, grading makes a judgment. Evaluation asks, What did I do well? What do I need to understand better? and What is my next step?

Evaluation should always be made *with* children or at least shared with them. One very important goal is to develop children's ability for self-evaluation.

## CLASSROOM PROFILES

As a summary, pictures of some classrooms at various levels have been drawn. We find that in the elementary school where children are learning to read through experience, each teacher values the individuality of the language expression which the child brings into the classroom. She knows that it is the raw material out of which refined language evolves. She believes that it is important to put as much emphasis on the child's improving his own language as on the child's ability to use other people's language. Both are important! She sees a language program as a total program rather than one broken into arbitrary parts. Reading is one language skill, but it cannot be distinguished from other language skills—speaking, listening, writing—when viewed in classrooms. This togetherness of skill development makes possible the continuing use of each child's own experience background and thinking as he grows toward maturity.

### Kindergarten

Looking in on Mrs. Davis' kindergarten you would see a teacher making use of the thinking powers of children. Each day she encourages some children to share their thoughts with the class and she records some of this with the individual child observing her or with the whole class watching as she does the writing. If a child seems to have a long, involved story, she lets him tell it all and then helps him select one or two of the most important statements to be written.

Children are helped to evaluate their own contributions by focusing on parts that are especially good, on progress they have made and sometimes on possible alternatives, what else they might have said, or how else they might have said it.

Children's creative efforts are given a place of honor in this classroom. Children share in the production and they are proud of their tackboards, chart racks and stories which accompany their paintings. The teacher constantly strengthens the link between oral language and reading. Through personal experiences, children know that "reading is just talk written down."

At this point in the school program the only person who is expected to read print is the teacher. She believes it is important that she read aloud each day something that the children have produced as well as something produced for children. One of the goals of this kindergarten teacher is that every child experiences authorship many times and that he have contacts with other kindergarten authors, as well as adult authors.

Another responsibility that this teacher feels deeply is that the experience background of children must be enriched and that each child's vocabulary for describing his experiences must be extended. Study trips, films, interest centers and group discussions all contribute to this vital objective.

### First Grade

Mrs. Clark knows that most of the children in her first grade class have had a rich language experience in kindergarten. When the children in her class dictate she expects them to make discriminating responses in regard to subject matter, choice of vocabulary, sentence structure, and the symbols of the language. As early as possible she expects children to begin recalling what they have dictated. As soon as a few are able to do this, she begins to develop a sight vocabulary based on the real language of the children in the classroom.

As the teacher takes dictation from a child, she talks about such things as letter formation, and the conventional symbols which represent the oral sounds which the child makes. She helps children discover words which are alike, words that begin alike and words that end alike. She is preparing children for independent writing at the same time she is helping them to recognize the common words in our language.

While the teacher is working with a small group or an individual child, other children are engaging in a variety of planned activities which will extend their experiences.* Some children manipulate materials at the science table; others create with paint or clay. One child may wish to be alone with his thoughts. Many children choose to read books which have been developed in their classroom. Others read books from the school library or those which they have brought from home. One can see that this classroom is truly a learning laboratory developed by both teacher and pupils.

Mrs. Clark considers that a major breakthrough occurs when an individual child wants to write his own story. She is sensitive to this time for every child. She encourages, gives recognition to and offers needed help for launching the child in his first independent writing.

The first child's breakthrough is sufficient motivation for many children to choose to do their own independent writing. As this occurs, the teachers and children develop many resources and procedures for writing and for reading the mate-

* For suggestions see Helen Fisher Darrow and R. Van Allen, *Independent Activities for Creative Learning* (New York, Bureau of Publications, Teachers College, Columbia University, 1961), 110 p.

rials which have been produced. They develop materials which
include:

- High frequency word lists.

- Word lists of common interest.

- Word lists on one topic.

- Picture dictionaries.

- Children's written material.

- Labels in the general environment.

They also know that they can have on-the-spot help from the
teacher and from other children.

At this point Mrs. Clark takes advantages of the self-motiva-
tion inherent in independent writing to work on the mastery
of the words most frequently used in all reading and writing.
Some techniques she includes are:

1. *The incomplete sentence* which the child finishes in his
   own unique way and with his own illustration. This procedure encourages diversity of ideas at the same time
   that the children are dealing with a common vocabulary.

2. *Making collections of children's writing* and binding
   them into books that can be read as free reading.

3. *Making resource books for social studies* to which all
   children contribute by adding illustrations and information.

As the children write they discover there are many things
about writing which they do not understand. Because they are
not threatened by failure to understand the common elements
of refinement, they are willing to discuss these refinements in
group seminars led by their teacher. The groups include only
those children who have and are recognizing the need for help
in understanding more about writing. The seminars deal with

topics such as capitalization, end of sentence punctuation, use of quotation marks, spelling, and phonics. This is the teachable moment for dealing with writing skills which relate to reading rather than the practice of interrupting the reading thought to teach these skills.

Children who have apparent difficulty comprehending reading material other than that which they have produced are scheduled to work with the teacher on an individual or small group basis. Their teacher selects published material that is designed to develop the skills which the children have not been able to understand and use. She seldom uses all the material in one book for direct teaching. Stories are selected because they provide material to teach specific skills. Some children may choose to read all of the stories in the book as a result of the work with the teacher, but this is not a requirement.

Some children need a great deal of direct teaching. Other children reach independence early and spend most of their reading time with materials selected at a library table.

**Third Grade**

Mr. Jones works in his third grade class to help children continue to develop their ability to read and to interest them with the content of a wide variety of books which are in their environment. These books provide stimulus for children's writing, as well as providing models of excellence in written expression.

The teacher's role is one of raising the children's level of awareness that there is more ahead for them. Participation in seminars which deal with areas such as style, form, enriched vocabulary, depth of meaning and word attack skills help children derive appreciation for the skills which other authors use as they write. At the same time children are developing functional skills which serve them as authors.

In this classroom, children not only *can* read with independence and comprehension, but they:

- Choose to read as a leisure time activity.

- Read as a means of finding answers to questions.

- Extend their information in areas of high interest through reading.

- Identify with good authorship to the point of being able to use excellence of style and form in their own writing.

As important as the skills being developed in Mr. Jones' class is the maturing of their attitude toward their responsibility as young citizens of a democratic society to share their own unique form of expression through speaking, writing and the publishing of what they write. These are the children who will be willing as well as be prepared to contribute effectively to a free society.

# 5

# GROUP AND INDIVIDUAL ACTIVITIES

Children who are learning to read through experience must live and work in a classroom environment which is rich with experiences. Only a part of the time can be spent in a program of direct instruction with the teacher. Provision must be made for children to work independently or with small groups on their own.

Activities which are suggested in this chapter are in addition to ones suggested in previous chapters. It is important to note at this point, however, that all activities, group or individual, which are included meet certain criteria which support the philosophy of involving children in the teaching-learning process. Each activity (1) requires the child to do productive thinking, (2) encourages the individual to reach toward the unknown, (3) creates new meanings out of old, (4) gives freedom of expression, (5) uses individual talents and skills and (6) contributes to personal satisfaction on the part of the children engaged in it. It is believed also that when children are in a climate of searching and discovering, they will suggest activities not preconceived by the teacher.

There are several sources of small group and individual activities which can be available all the time. It is the responsibility of the teacher to provide the sources rather than to provide the specific activity for a group or individual. Choice of activities is an essential ingredient in the program of learning through experience. Some examples of sources are:

1. *The room environment.* When interest centers have been organized in the classroom, children can use the materials in them. A writing center with paper, pencils of all colors, word lists, and suggested titles will attract many children. A reading corner or an arithmetic center will encourage individual discovery and experimentation. A science corner which changes frequently can be a basic source of many activities. An art table with all kinds of media offers opportunity for self-expression. A music table with tone bells and other musical instruments may be noisy, but there are times when it can be used by children to explore new musical learnings.

2. *Extension of group experiences.* When a poem or story is read and gets a favorable response from children, a variety of activities which may last for days can be planned by the children. They can paint scenes, make a movie or TV or prepare a bulletin board with cut-out characters.

When a group which is getting acquainted with the school visits the cafeteria, activities might evolve which would result in the building of a cafeteria for dramatic play. Some children would plan the cafeteria, others might make "play food" from clay or with paper cut-outs. Others could plan the management of the cafeteria.

A group discussion on word sounds or meanings can result in activities such as:

- Collecting concrete objects for a chart or exhibit (things made of cotton, spices, insects).

- Developing word games to extend and practice the learnings.

A film on cloud formation might lead to activities involving:

- A bulletin board with various kinds of clouds made from paper or cotton.

- A daily record for a week of the kinds of cloud formations observed.

- Descriptions of "what the clouds make me think of."

3. *Teacher demonstrations and planning.* Sometimes teachers use a "here's how" period to show children a new art medium, a new technique for binding a book, some unusual way to write riddles, or the use of new science equipment. In this way the teacher is helping children gain confidence in handling materials for themselves. From such a beginning it is hoped that each child will discover his own ways of handling materials.

Group and individual activities require teacher-pupil planning. Time must be given to clarify plans for the day. Time is also required for evaluation of accomplishments and sharing of ideas. It is only when children have a part in describing the "what," "why," and "how" of daily activities that they can feel a personal satisfaction in taking responsibility for them.

### SUGGESTED ACTIVITIES

#### For the Total Class

*Building with words.* Make word pyramids by beginning at the top rather than at the bottom. Write a noun on the chalkboard, then choose appropriate words to build the pyramid.

*Taking dictation.* Let the class play a game of being secretaries. The teacher dictates short letters to pupils.

*Story train.* Place five chairs at the front of the room, one behind the other. The pupil in the first chair is the engineer. He starts a story by saying, "On my way home I saw a rabbit (or something else)." Those in chairs two, three, and four each make a complete sentence about the thing the engineer sees. The child in the last chair repeats the whole story, just as

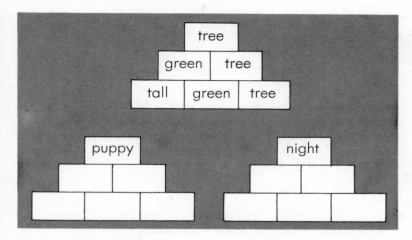

the others told it. This activity is used to help children be more observing, to tell more than one thing about what they see, to make complete sentences and to be good listeners.

*Making Class Books—Dictating.* When all or a large number of children are painting and dictating on the same general topic or about a common experience, paper should be pro-

vided that is not too large to bind into books as several stories are completed. Children may use crayons or tempera paint to illustrate their ideas. The teacher then groups the children in small groups of eight to ten to dictate their stories to her. She arranges them so they can observe her as she records the speech of the "storyteller." The story may be written at the bottom of the picture. With this plan the children should be encouraged to fold a space at the top or bottom of the paper

where they will not paint. Or the book may be made up with illustrations on one page and stories on the opposite page.

After the stories and pictures are complete, they are bound into books which the teacher reads to the total class and then puts on the library table for the children to enjoy. Some classes exchange books. Others invite first and second grade classes to their room for a story time when the teacher reads books which have been "authored" by kindergarten children.

On Saturday we
went to Disneyland.
My favorite ride
was on the submar-
ine. I thought it
was real.
                    Bobby

**In the Writing Center**

*Book Jacket Stories.* Use book jackets from the library by pinning several on a bulletin board with a caption:

- Choose a Book Jacket
- Use the Same Title
- Write Your Own Story

After several books have been written with book jacket covers, the books might be brought into the reading center. Children can compare and contrast the stories they wrote with those of the original author.

*Words We Use.* Make beginning lists of words that will be used in writing as a total class activity. Ask children to add to the lists as they use other words. Encourage children to refer to the lists as they write.

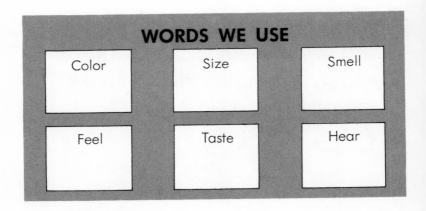

**WORDS WE USE**

| Color | Size | Smell |
| Feel | Taste | Hear |

*Blank Books.* Make blank books with attractive covers and inviting titles. Invite children to add illustrations and stories to the books. Some suggested titles are:

- *Toys That Go*
- *Some Things Are Round*
- *What I Discovered*
- *All Around Our Neighborhood*
- *Accidents Will Happen*
- *Jasper and Casper*
- *Our Caterpillars*

Older children might have an editor or an editorial committee for each of the books. A child would submit his story to the editor for approval and revision before copying it into the book. Children can work in pairs as author and illustrator.

*Making Story Titles.* Encourage children to make catchy titles for their stories. This can be done by placing several pictures on a bulletin board. Ask pupils to add story titles under each picture. First, one word titles are added; next, two words—two words that rhyme; then three or more words.

*Individual Writing.* The teacher can place 15 to 20 words on the chalkboard. Some are basic sight words and some are from current interests of the group. Children, on their own time, can make as many complete sentences as possible using just those words.

*Writing Handbook.* In a classroom where writing is to be emphasized, each child should begin a personal *Writing Handbook* that will contain help which is needed all the time in writing. From time to time children will suggest pages for the handbook that others will want to use. Some of the beginning pages might be "A List of Words Most Frequently Used in Writing." *This list should be provided by the teacher to every child*. Some good lists are the *Madden-Carlson, Dolch, Thorndike* or *Rinsland*. Children should become very much aware of the vocabulary on these lists and not waste time looking for such words in dictionaries. By the end of the second grade,

## My "Said" Words

1. answered
2. barked
3. called
4. demanded
5. screamed
6. whispered
7.
8.
9.
10.
11.
12.

## My "Color" Words

1. bright
2. dim
3. glisten
4. olive green
5. snow white
6. dark
7.
8.
9.
10.
11.
12.

## My "Size" Words

1. tiny
2. huge
3. tremendous
4. large
5. thin
6. thick
7. long
8:
9.
10.
11.
12.

## My "Feeling" Words

1. happy
2. sad
3. calm
4. quiet
5. nervous
6. jittery
7. awful
8.
9.
10.
11.
12.

some children will be able to read and spell all of these words at sight.

Other pages might be "My Said List," "My Color Words," "My Size Words" and other lists that make ready reference for children who are writing conversation and description. The children add to these lists as they read and write. They should be encouraged to get new words from good authors.

### In the Music Center

*Name This Tune.* Provide a table with a set of tone bells and a small tack board where children can transcribe the beginning measures or the main theme of a composition for others to "Name This Tune." A book of familiar songs might be provided as suggestions.

*What Am I?* Children who are learning to read music will enjoy contributing to a "What Am I" bulletin board or chart. They can add any new sign or symbol which they encounter. Children who are interested can keep a personal check list with the answers.

*Make a Tune.* On a table with an autoharp and tone bells, the teacher or a child can leave bits of poetry which they have found or composed and invite someone to make a tune. A collection of the tunes will make a good class book.

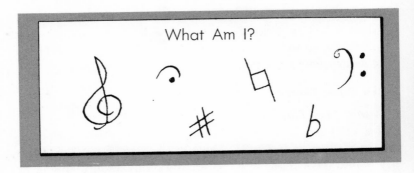

### In the Reading Center

*Expanding Vocabulary.* On the chart place a series of pictures with common nouns and leave space for children to add other names for the same things as they find them in their reading.

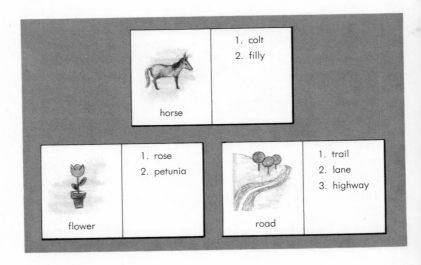

Another variation of the same activity is to make the chart with pictures and common names and invite children to add descriptive words which they encounter in reading such as:

*Follow-Up Activities.* A child can prepare an activity page for a story he has read. The teacher duplicates some of the pages and places them with the book for other children to complete when they read the story. Children can be helped to make better questions through evaluation.

*Recognizing Beginning Sounds.* The teacher can put a large piece of paper on a wall on which children can copy words which they discover that begin with a particular sound. The letters can be changed from time to time.

*Retelling Stories.* After a story is read to the class, children can illustrate a favorite part of it to pin on a bulletin board.

Children may retell a story by drawing three or more pictures about the story and numbering them to show the sequence of events.

## Just for Fun · Pages 12-15

Name of story _____

Who looked out the window? _____

Who was in the tree? _____

Who watched Mother? _____

prepared by Diane

### Words that begin with

| *b* | *d* | *f* | *g* | *s* | *w* |
|-----|-----|-----|-----|-----|-----|
|     |     |     |     |     |     |

*Recording Stories.* If a tape recorder is available in the class-room, a good activity to continue throughout the year is to encourage children to read original stories on tape. Children will usually observe the sign, "Quiet, Please, Recording in Progress," if a screened-off place can be provided. At a special time, such as once a week, the tapes made during the week can be played to the class for their listening time. Children like to surprise others with stories. They usually do a better job of oral reading as a result of this kind of experience.

*Recognizing Vowel Sounds.* The teacher can put a large sheet of paper on a wall with headings which invite children to share their discoveries about vowel sounds.

| LONG AND SHORT VOWELS WE HAVE DISCOVERED | | | | | | | | | |
|---|---|---|---|---|---|---|---|---|---|
| long $\bar{a}$ | short $\breve{a}$ | long $\bar{e}$ | short $\breve{e}$ | long $\bar{\imath}$ | short $\breve{\imath}$ | long $\bar{o}$ | short $\breve{o}$ | long $\bar{u}$ | short $\breve{u}$ |
| | | | | | | | | | |

### In the Art Center

*Models.* Make models of vehicles, buildings, bridges, from wood, paper, metal. Ideas may come from listening to stories or from reading.

*Miniatures.* Construct a setting, in miniature, for a story which can be told to the class.

*Puppets.* Make puppets of characters in a story for telling to the class.

*Painting Sentences.* Place sentences at the top or bottom of newsprint that is to be used at the easel. Let the child select a sentence which he can read and illustrate. Examples are:

- See all the fish.

- I like animals.

- See my cat.
- There are five pumpkins.
- I used four colors.

*Bulletin Board Display*. Children, with the teacher, can select a broad topic such as:

- Our Pets
- Good Breakfast Foods
- Plants in Our Yards
- Insects We Have Seen
- Halloween Fun
- Toys with Wheels

Each child is encouraged to add an illustration to the board. He is to do this on his own time. If he can do so, he should label his contribution.

### In the Science Corner

*Things We Know*. Several folders can be placed in the science corner with titles that suggest information which can be added by anyone, such as:

- *What We See at Night*
- *Things We Know About Air*
- *Things We Know About Water*
- *How the Sun Helps Us*
- *Animals That Live in Water*

Children add statements and illustrations to the folders. Later, these can be compiled as a class book.

*Discoveries.* Provide objects on the science table such as a magnifying glass, globe, magnet, levers, plants, human anatomy model.

Prepare and leave on the table a booklet that has space for individuals to write their "discoveries" and sign their names. This information can later be organized and used for class discussions in which the discovery can be elaborated.

*Bulletin Board Display.* A bulletin board should be reserved to display information about wild plants and animals. The teacher can begin the bulletin board with leading questions such as: "How Long Do Animals Live?" "How Long Do Plants Live?" "How Do Animals and Plants Differ?" Children will add their illustrations and information to the bulletin board. When a board is filled with information, the children might like to take it down and make the pictures and stories into a book.

*Making Classification Games.* Children can make games with pictures or words which will help them review the information they are dealing with in a study such as wildlife. A master card can be developed by the teacher such as:

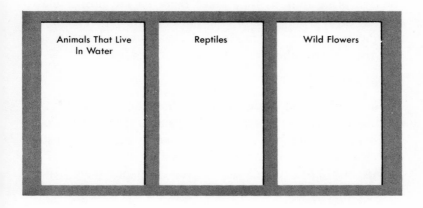

| Animals That Live In Water | Reptiles | Wild Flowers |

Blank cards of tagboard can be provided for children to use in making their own cards. As children make word cards or picture cards, they can place them in the appropriate place. These can be used as games for other children to play. Let children suggest the kinds of games that can be played.

*"All About" Books.* Some children who read well may want to make a special study of some animal or plant. For those who are interested in this activity the teacher can help the children develop a list of pages that can be included in every book. Then each child will be encouraged to add others to his individual book. Such pages might include: what the animals eat, types of homes, value to man, kinds of teeth, kinds of feet, habits, length of life, care when kept as a pet, care of the young, care when kept in a zoo and others. "All About Snakes," "All About Frogs," "All About Rabbits," and any other animal or plant can be a topic of special interest. These books can become reference material and reading material for members of the class who can not handle usual reference material.

*Collections.* A collection of some sort should be in progress all the time. Shells, leaves, pictures, buttons, etc., are good for young children. The teacher with a group of children should develop the format for each collection. For example, when children bring buttons they place them on the proper classification card. One or more children can make a matching or classification game by mixing all the buttons together and then trying to put them back on the correct card.

**This and That Corner**

*Guess What?* Put objects in boxes that can be sealed. Invite children to guess what is in the box. Encourage them to shake, smell, weigh, and get other clues before making a list of guesses to read before opening the box.

*This and That.* Cardboard boxes or paper bags can be arranged with all kinds of helpful materials. The material can

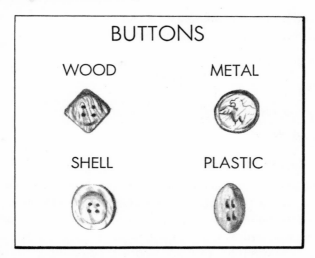

be added to by teacher and children. Bags might contain, for example, word collections—words, letters, children's names. Various styles of type, but always in large print, can be made available. Pupils use the words to:

- Make scrapbooks using pasted on words with own illustrations.

- Construct sentences by selecting words to paste on the paper.

- Select words for a spelling list.

- Place rhyming words on flannel board.

*Messenger Service.* Use a "message file" to write get-well messages or birthday greetings for friends. Each child puts a card with his name, address, phone number, and birthday in the file.

*At the Chalkboard.* Children should be encouraged to write

and sketch at the chalkboard. Headings that are inviting will
attract children to use the chalkboard, such as:

- A Poem I like

- My Best Story

- Good Writing

- New Words

### In the Publishing Corner

*Publishing a Newspaper or Magazine.* Most primary grade
children enjoy publishing a newspaper or a magazine. This
can be done on the children's own time if there are two or more
children who are advanced enough in reading and writing to
take the responsibility of being editor the first weeks of school.

In preparation for the publication, the teacher brings to
the classroom some copies of newspapers and children's
magazines and discusses their development and use. In the
class discussion she points out that some of the articles are
reports on news in the community and the world, some are
about interesting announcements of things to happen later.
There are stories, both real and imaginary, puzzles, riddles
and jokes, comic strips, pictures and many other kinds of
writing that will be of interest to readers.

With this kind of background she can help the class get
organized for developing a publication. They will need an
editor and an assistant editor who will have the responsibility
of getting the publication organized, edited and printed. The
editors need a small corner of the room in which to work.
They can set up their office so that children will know where
and how to submit their material for the publication.

One second grade class published *The Rocket.* It was a
magazine of 15 to 20 pages each time it was printed. The class
decided that each issue would contain certain sections: Real
Stories, Imaginary Stories, Poems, Interviews of Interesting

People, Riddles and Jokes, Puzzles, Arithmetic Problems and Games, Word Games, Spelling Games, Science Articles, Science Fiction, and Sports. Each new staff could add other sections.

The editors made folders for each category and children were asked to write their articles at school or at home and place their stories and pictures in the proper folder. No class

time was designated for this activity. The editors would keep check on the progress of their publication and would send some of their reporters to collect material for sections that were not developing. The reporters could write or find someone else who would write for the section. An editorial committee would then check all of the contributions for needed revision. Most of the time they would do the minor revision, but if major changes were to be made, the author was called for a conference. Sometimes an illustration needed to be reduced in size, sometimes an article needed five or six more lines to fill up the space and sometimes an article would be too long. One thing that the teacher insisted on was that all contributions be used in the publication.

When the publication was ready to be printed, the school secretary cut the stencils, leaving space for children to add their illustrations and sign their articles. The magazines were distributed free to members of the class and sold for ten cents to other children and adults who wanted them. In this way the cost of the extra stencils and paper was taken care of and at the same time the accounting for the money was a good project for the children.

### Writing Resources in the Classroom

*Lists of High Frequency Words.* As the children are introduced to words through incomplete sentences, the words should be kept in the classroom environment for future reference in independent writing. These may be written on the chalkboard, printed on a bulletin board chart, or be made into "word ladders" by stringing the word cards on long shoestrings.

As a guide to the selection of additional words which are of high frequency in our language, the *Madden-Carlson* list of 250 words of highest frequency is included in Appendix *A*. This list is also useful as a guide in developing incomplete sentences for other units.

*Dictated Stories.* Stories that are dictated to accompany easel paintings can be kept on a chart rack or in books. Children will refer to stories they already know for words they need in their stories.

*Labels.* Labels around the room give some words that are useful. "Color" words and "size" words are especially helpful to beginning authors.

*Class Books.* As books are developed on topics of interest to the class, they become useful as word sources. Many children will remember words that have been dictated in the stories.

*Special Lists.* Every two or three days the class might discuss a topic of current interest. Out of the discussion might come four or five words that several children will want to use in their writing. These can be written on the chalkboard.

*Alphabet Models.* In addition to the alphabet models usually found above the chalkboard, teachers who expect children to write every day should provide individual guides with markings which help children to develop proper writing habits. The individual alphabet models should have letters about the same size as the ones the children will be writing.

# Appendix A

## BASIC WORD LIST

250 Words of Highest Frequency in Our Language
Selected by Richard Madden and Thorsten Carlson

| | | | | | |
|---|---|---|---|---|---|
| a | be | Christmas | enough | give | house |
| about | beautiful | city | ever | go | how |
| after | because | cold | every | going | I |
| again | bed | come | father | good | if |
| all | been | comes | few | got | in |
| | | | | | |
| along | before | coming | find | great | into |
| also | best | could | fire | had | is |
| always | better | country | first | hard | it |
| am | big | day | five | happy | just |
| an | book | days | for | has | keep |
| | | | | | |
| and | boy | dear | found | have | kind |
| another | boys | did | four | he | know |
| any | brother | didn't | friend | heard | large |
| are | but | do | from | help | last |
| around | by | dog | fun | her | left |
| | | | | | |
| as | called | don't | gave | here | let |
| asked | came | door | get | him | letter |
| at | can | down | getting | his | like |
| away | car | each | girl | home | little |
| back | children | eat | girls | hope | live |

129

| | | | | | |
|---|---|---|---|---|---|
| lived | never | people | stay | today | well |
| long | new | place | still | told | went |
| look | next | play | summer | too | were |
| looked | nice | pretty | sure | took | what |
| made | night | put | take | town | when |
| | | | | | |
| make | no | ran | teacher | tree | where |
| man | not | read | tell | two | which |
| many | now | ready | than | until | while |
| may | of | right | that | up | white |
| me | off | room | the | us | who |
| | | | | | |
| men | old | said | their | use | will |
| money | on | saw | them | used | winter |
| more | once | say | then | very | with |
| morning | one | school | there | want | work |
| most | only | see | these | wanted | would |
| | | | | | |
| mother | or | she | they | was | write |
| much | other | should | thing | water | year |
| must | our | side | things | way | years |
| my | out | small | think | we | you |
| name | over | snow | this | week | your |
| | | so | thought | | |
| | | some | three | | |
| | | something | through | | |
| | | soon | time | | |
| | | started | to | | |

# Appendix B

## RELATIONSHIP OF COMMUNICATION SKILLS

Bond, Guy L., and others, Pre-Primers, *Three of Us, Play with Us, Fun with Us,* with Teacher's Guide. Chicago, Lyons & Carnahan, 1954, pp. 18-19.

> *Language Facility.* Language facility is one of the more important readiness factors that are definitely trainable. Upon entering school, the children have come from home situations which differ widely in the quality of language and in the opportunity to use language. There are many children who have not had stories read to them or told to them and they may lack story sense; some children lack sentence sense; some have difficulty in expressing their own ideas with clarity; some have inaccurate pronunciation and articulation; many children have never had the opportunity to express themselves to groups of children. All children in the first grade will profit from activities which enable them to use language, to tell stories, to formulate sequence of ideas, and to anticipate the outcomes of stories.

McKee, Paul, and others, Teacher's Manual for *Tip.* Boston, Houghton Mifflin, 1957, pp. 4-5.

> *The Language Arts.* The modern elementary school provides instruction in a group of subjects or activities commonly

called the *language arts.* These arts are (1) *speaking,* including the school subjects known as composition, speech, and
grammar, (2) *writing,* including the school subjects known
as composition, spelling, grammar, and handwriting, (3)
*listening,* and (4) *reading.* The fundamental aim of instruction in the language arts is to help the child acquire the
language abilities he needs if he is to communicate with others
and to think clearly about his own problems. *Speaking* and
*writing* are taught so that the child may learn to transmit his
meanings and his feelings effectively to others and to think
efficiently about his problems. *Listening* and *reading* are
taught so that the child may learn to construct the meanings
and feelings presented to him by others in their speaking and
writing and so that he may think about those meanings and
feelings in relation to his own problems.

*Order of Development.* The four language arts have close
relationships with one another that need to be considered in
making instructional programs in any one of them.

Russell, David H., and Ousley, Odille, *Manual for Teaching
the Pre-Primer Program.* Boston, Ginn, 1957, p. 8.

*Learning to Read Is Learning to Communicate.* Reading is
one of the language arts, that important group of human
activities concerned with the communication of ideas. Communication involves giving ideas to others as in speaking,
oral reading, and writing. It also involves receiving ideas from
others, as in listening, observing, and reading silently. Reading, then, involves both the giving and the receiving of ideas.
The effectiveness of oral reading of a story, poem, or passage;
the adequacy of silent reading may be measured by the speed
and exactness with which one gets the facts, the main ideas,
or the implied outcomes from the printed page. As one of
the language arts, the child's reading is closely connected to
his oral language, his writing, and his other work with words.

Sheldon, William D., and others, Teacher's Manual, *At Home, Here and Near, Here and Away.* Boston, Allyn & Bacon, 1957, pp. 3-4.

*Reading and the Language Arts.* Reading is one of four basic language processes, along with listening, speaking, and writing. Reading instruction is based upon the listening and speaking skills which the children bring to each reading level. Phonetic principles are developed from a child's ability to distinguish the sounds of the words in his speaking and listening vocabularies, and new concepts are developed from the ideas and impressions contained in his vocabulary of familiar words. Also, reading skill is of major importance in developing the ability to spell and to write clearly, interestingly, and knowledgeably—for writing skill depends largely upon the extension of word knowledge through reading. This is particularly true in the specific subject matter areas where the technical vocabulary and basic concepts are not met in ordinary conversation, in or out of the classroom.

Studies have shown that the acquisition of such skills as correct usage, punctuation, capitalization, and spelling are directly related to reading ability. These relationships are found not only on the primary level but in junior and senior high schools as well. As children grow in reading ability, language leaves the reader richer in terminology and in mode of expression. He not only learns new words but also how to use them.

Reading, inseparable from other language processes, is best taught as part of the whole area of language development. The interrelationships are such that each aspect of language is dependent upon every other.

Stauffer, Russell G., and others, Teachers Edition for *Come Here, Stop and Look, Go up.* New York, Holt, Rinehart and Winston, 1960, p. 2.

Reading is one method of communication. Although reading is commonly taught as a 'separate' subject, teachers recognize that the communication skills are interrelated. They supplement and complement one another. A child gains reading power by writing. He improves his writing by reading. He learns to talk by listening. He develops listening skills by speaking.

Strickland, Ruth G., "Reading in Its Setting—The Language Arts." *The Packet,* Vol. 15, No. 1, (Spring, 1960), Boston, D. C. Heath.

There appears to be a close relationship between the majority of the sentences a child uses in his speech and his comprehension and interpretation of sentences on a printed page. The more the early experiences in learning to read utilize what the child already knows in ways which he clearly understands, the easier it will be for him to learn to read. This means, among other things, that the closer the reading material used in the early stages of introducing a child to reading approximates the child's own talk the easier it will be for him to comprehend and make a part of himself the essential process of reading. . . .

Let me carry this point further. Probably the best method that has been devised for inducting children into reading is through putting their own talk into symbol form on chalkboard or chart and in little booklets of their own making.

Tinker, Miles A., *Teaching Elementary Reading.* New York, Appleton-Century-Crofts, 1952, p. 11.

*Steps in learning to read.* In the beginning, learning to read is learning that symbols (queer, senseless-looking marks to the child) stand for speech. He learns to say the word that stands for a particular printed or written mark. Whether the child speaks the word to himself or out loud, reading at this stage means saying the correct word. When the correct words are spoken, they occur in a familiar sequence that has meaning for him because of his previous experience in understanding and using speech. In other words, the essential basis for learning to read is an adequate background of speaking and understanding of speech sounds.

# Appendix C

## OBSERVATION CHART

Here is a streamlined version of the observation outline on pp. 16 to 21. This may be duplicated so that teachers have a copy for each child with whom they are working. As much space may be left between headings as they may need. Teachers may wish to refer to the original as they are observing.

1. Is the child's life comfortable enough so he can give attention to school learnings?

    *a.* Evidence of physical ill health?

    *b.* Evidence of mental ill health?

    *c.* Evidence of high anxiety, tension, unhappiness?

2. Are his "intake" abilities functioning adequately?

    *a.* Inadequate vision?

    *b.* Inadequate hearing?

    *c.* Inadequate physical participation?

    *d.* What kinds of things does he ignore?

3. Are his "expressive" abilities functioning adequately?

    *a.* Does he express himself in complete thought units?

    *b.* Is his expression relevant?

    *c.* Does he contribute to group discussion?

    *d.* Does he converse freely?

    *e.* Does he enunciate clearly?

    *f.* Does he use correct English?

4. Are school learnings important to him?

    *a.* What are parent's goals?

    *b.* Does he use books?

    *c.* Does he show normal curiosity?

    *d.* What kind of activities hold his attention?

5. Is he confident of school success?

    *a.* What evidence is there of his self-concept?

    *b.* Does his self confidence vary with different areas?

# Appendix D

## TESTS

The following is data needed for ordering any of the tests listed in Chapter 2:

*California Test of Mental Maturity,* 1957, Preprimary 70 min., primary 90 min., $5.25 per 35 tests, 50¢ per specimen set. California Test Bureau, Del Monte Research Park, Monterey, California.

*Davis-Eells Test of General Intelligence and Problem Solving,* 1953, 60 min. in 2 sessions for grade 1, $3.70 per 35 tests, 35¢ per specimen set. Harcourt, Brace & World, New York.

*Goodenough Draw-a-Man Test,* 1926. 10 min., $1.50 per 35 children's drawing sheets, $3.25 per manual, no specimen set. Harcourt, Brace & World, New York.

*Group Test of Learning Capacity: The Dominion Tests,* 1956, 50 min. in two sessions, $1.80 per 25 tests, 45¢ per specimen set. Guidance Center, Ontario College of Education, University of Toronto, 371 Bloor St. West, Toronto 5, Ontario, Canada.

*IPAT Culture Free Intelligence Test,* 1950, 30 min., $3.50 per 25 tests, $3.00 per set of cards for classification test, 75¢ per specimen set. Institute for Personality and Ability Testing, 1602 Coronado Drive, Champaign, Illinois.

*Kuhlmann-Anderson Intelligence Tests,* 1952, 45-50 min., $2.40 per 25 tests, $1.00 per specimen set. Personnel Press, Inc., 188 Nassau St., Princeton, New Jersey.

*Lorge-Thorndike Intelligence Tests,* 1957, 35 min. in 2 or 3 ses-

sions, $3.00 per 35 tests, 60¢ per specimen set. Houghton
Mifflin Co., 2 Park St., Boston 7, Massachusetts.

*SRA Primary Mental Abilities,* 1953, 60-80 min. in two sessions,
$3.00 per 20 tests, 50¢ per specimen. Science Research Asso-
ciates, 259 East Erie, Chicago 11, Illinois.

*American School Reading Readiness Test,* 1955, 45 min., $2.75
per 25 tests, 35¢ per specimen set. Public School Publishing
Co., 345 Calhoun St., Cincinnati 19, Ohio.

*Group Test of Reading Readiness: The Dominion Tests,* 1955, 30-
50 min. in two sessions, $1.70 per 20 tests, 25¢ per set of 10
flash cards, 70¢ per specimen set. Guidance Center, Ontario
College of Education, University of Toronto, 371 Bloor St.
West, Toronto 5, Ontario, Canada.

*Lee-Clark Reading Readiness Test,* 1951, 20 min., $3.15 per 35
tests, 25¢ per specimen set. California Test Bureau, Del
Monte Research Park, Monterey, California.

*Metropolitan Readiness Tests,* 1933, 1950, 65-75 min., $2.25 per
25 tests, 35¢ per specimen set. Harcourt, Brace & World,
New York.

# Index